SCHOOL BULLYING

OXFORD WORKSHOP SERIES:

SCHOOL SOCIAL WORK ASSOCIATION OF AMERICA

Series Advisory Board

Evidence-Based Practice in School Mental Health
James C. Raines

The Domains and Demands of School Social Work Practice:
A Guide to Working Effectively with Students, Families, and Schools
Michael S. Kelly

Solution-Focused Brief Therapy in Schools:
A 360-Degree View of Research and Practice
Michael S. Kelly, Johnny S. Kim, and Cynthia Franklin

A New Model of School Discipline:
Engaging Students and Preventing Behavior Problems
David R. Dupper

Truancy Prevention and Intervention:
A Practical Guide
Lynn Bye, Michelle E. Alvarez, Janet Haynes, and Cindy E. Sweigart

Ethical Decision Making in School Mental Health
James C. Raines and Nic T. Dibble

Functional Behavioral Assessment:
A Three-Tiered Prevention Model
Kevin J. Filter and Michelle E. Alvarez

School Bullying:
New Perspectives on a Growing Problem
David R. Dupper

SCHOOL BULLYING

New Perspectives on a Growing Problem

David R. Dupper

OXFORD WORKSHOP SERIES

OXFORD
UNIVERSITY PRESS

OXFORD
UNIVERSITY PRESS

Oxford University Press is a department of the University of Oxford.
It furthers the University's objective of excellence in research, scholarship,
and education by publishing worldwide.

Oxford   New York
Auckland   Cape Town   Dar es Salaam   Hong Kong   Karachi
Kuala Lumpur   Madrid   Melbourne   Mexico City   Nairobi
New Delhi   Shanghai   Taipei   Toronto

With offices in
Argentina   Austria   Brazil   Chile   Czech   Republic   France   Greece
Guatemala   Hungary   Italy   Japan   Poland   Portugal   Singapore
South Korea   Switzerland   Thailand   Turkey   Ukraine   Vietnam

Oxford is a registered trade mark of Oxford University Press in the UK and certain other
countries.

Published in the United States of America by
Oxford University Press
198 Madison Avenue, New York, NY 10016

Library of Congress Cataloging-in-Publication Data
Dupper, David R.
School bullying : new perspectives on a
growing problem / David R. Dupper.
p. cm.
(Oxford workshop series)
Includes bibliographical references and index.
ISBN 978–0–19–985959–7 (pbk : alk. paper)
1. Bullying in schools United States   2. Bullying in schools
United States Prevention.   1. Title.
LB3013.32.D87 2012
371.5'8—dc23
2012025240

Printed in the United States of America

Contents

Preface

Bullying is one of the most prevalent and insidious forms of violence in schools today. A recent study by the Josephson Institute of Ethics reported that nearly half of the 43,000 students in their sample stated they were bullied, teased, or taunted in a way that seriously upset them in the past year (2010). The Centers for Disease Control and Prevention (CDC) has identified cyberbullying as an emerging adolescent health issue. Rather than a "rite of passage" and "normal part of growing up," bullying must be viewed for what it is: a systematic abuse of power.

Bullying impacts the learning environment of schools in profound ways. Victims of chronic bullying have poorer grades, increased rates of truancy, increased rates of dropping out, loss of self-esteem, and feelings of isolation and depression, and some even attempt suicide. Students who witness bullying are often intimidated and fearful that it will eventually happen to them. As a result, witnesses may also perform poorly in the classroom because their attention is focused on how to avoid being harmed rather than their schoolwork. Victims may also become bullies themselves and perpetuate a destructive cycle of violence.

Unfortunately, "many educators and other professionals lack sufficient understanding of the phenomenon of bullying and of best practices in bullying prevention and intervention" (Olweus & Limber, 2010, p. 132). Nearly half of school social work respondents in a recent survey did not feel equipped to deal with cyberbullying (Slovak & Singer, 2011). This volume was written to address this knowledge gap among school professionals and others who want to more fully understand the complex nature of the bullying phenomenon. This volume discusses school bullying from an ecological systems perspective that broadens the conceptualization of bullying and enlarges the potential targets for intervention. It expands the current discussion of bullying in schools to include all the ways in which power is misused and abused in schools including adult–student relationships. It frames bullying within the larger cultural context of the United States and incorporates international perspectives on bullying. While some of these international perspectives may not be applicable in addressing bullying in the United States, an international perspective allows us to broaden our conceptualization of bullying and allows for creative approaches to a seemingly intractable and complex problem. This volume utilizes a whole-school approach as a framework for developing and implementing comprehensive interventions to combat bullying. A whole-school approach seeks to engage all members of the school community (e.g., students, teachers, staff, parents, community members) in developing a common vision and a commitment to combat all forms of bullying in schools. A whole-school approach seeks to change the entire culture and climate of the school.

This volume highlights the latest research findings on the nature and extent of all forms of bullying in schools today, including dispelling myths about bullies and focusing on the increasingly important role that peer witnesses play in exacerbating as well as combating bullying in schools. A unique feature of this volume is the discussion of several "under-the-radar" forms of bullying in schools (i.e., religious bullying, bullying by teachers and other adults in schools) and the unique political challenges in assessing and combating these largely unacknowledged forms of bullying in today's U.S. schools. Perhaps most important, this volume discusses specific steps, based on best practices, that can be taken to combat all forms of bullying in schools in as comprehensive a manner as possible.

In Chapter 1, I lay the framework for the rest of this volume by conceptualizing and discussing the bullying phenomenon from an ecological-systems perspective. Bullying is a complex phenomenon that defies simple explanations and simple solutions, and the ecological-systems perspective is a very useful framework for increasing our understanding of bullying in all of its complexity. An ecological-systems perspective of bullying, which has begun to receive empirical support, allows us to develop interventions based on this complexity. I argue that bullying in our schools is a reflection of bullying in our culture and that our youth are receiving mixed and confusing messages about bullying behavior from adults. I discuss a "culture of bullying" that exists in some schools and serves to normalize bullying within that school. I also talk about how the physiological and psychological changes that mark early adolescence exacerbate the potential for bullying and explains a spike in bullying behaviors in 6th grade followed by a steady decline in later grades.

In Chapter 2, I define bullying in all of its forms as a "systematic abuse of power." I point out that it is important to be able to distinguish between bullying and other types of peer conflict, such as teasing. I emphasize that bullying is a specific type of aggression that involves an imbalance of power where the bully consciously intends to harm his or her victim physically and/or psychologically and has the power and the means to do so. I discuss recent research findings on those individual characteristics, family characteristics, and a number of school characteristics that have been associated with bullying. Bullying appears to be widespread in our public schools today, but it is also important to note that bullying statistics may seriously underestimate the problem. I point out that bullying is no longer viewed as a normative phase that most children outgrow but a serious problem with short- and long-term consequences. In fact, recent neuroscience research findings provide evidence that the impact of psychological forms of bullying can be as devastating for the victim as physical abuse. I also discuss research on "popular bullies" and emerging evidence that bullying is increasingly being viewed as a strategy for gaining or maintaining status among one's peers. I examine the critical role that peer witnesses play in bullying incidents. I also discuss how teachers and administrators often underestimate or downplay the extent to which bullying is a problem in their school as well as the role that they can play to prevent bullying.

In Chapter 3, I provide a detailed, up-to-date discussion of what we know about cyberbullying and what can be done to combat it. Cyberbullying differs in important ways from face-to-face bullying and has taken bullying to new levels of cruelty and brutality. I argue that interventions to combat cyberbullying must take into account these important differences. For example, teens may be more reluctant to report instances of electronic bullying since a report of electronic bullying may result in a restriction in cell phone or Internet use. The primary challenge facing educators in combating cyberbullying is finding a balance between freedom of speech and "the darker side of digital communication." I point out that empathy training appears to be an important component of any effort to combat cyberbullying.

In Chapter 4, I provide a detailed discussion of the latest research findings on the bullying of lesbian, gay, bisexual, and transgender (LGBT) students in schools. I discuss the unrelenting bullying and harassment experienced by LGBT students by their peers and the fact that school employees often do little or nothing to stop antigay behavior when they witness it. I discuss several concrete steps that can be taken by school officials to minimize antigay bullying in schools and also acknowledge the substantial opposition from moral conservatives in combating LGBT bullying in schools. Unfortunately, school personnel are often caught in the middle of this intense political and religious battle. While most teachers want to protect LGBT students from being bullied, teachers also do not want to violate the rights of morally conservative parents. In this chapter, I also discuss sexual bullying and sexual harassment, defined as any form of physical or nonphysical bullying using a person's sexuality or gender as a weapon by boys or girls toward other boys or girls. By viewing sexual bullying as harassment, school districts can take specific actions based on the federal definition of sexual harassment and the rights of students under Title IX. I highlight several programs that show promise in reducing sexual bullying and harassment in schools.

In Chapter 5, I discuss "under-the-radar" forms of bullying, namely, religious bullying and bullying by teachers and other adults. A number of case studies and legal briefs suggest that religious bullying in U.S. public schools may be a much broader and more pervasive form of bullying than many currently acknowledge. Religious bullying has been defined as repeated acts of aggression in which the power of institutional religion is used to mock, humiliate, or threaten others who do not share the same religious beliefs or practices. I point out that the central legal issue facing school officials is balancing the rights of free speech (including religious expression) as well as protecting students from being coerced by others to accept certain religious (or antireligious) beliefs. I discuss several recommendations for increasing religious tolerance in U.S. public schools. In this chapter I also discuss a largely unacknowledged and often hidden form of bullying in schools—teachers who bully students. A teacher-bully is a teacher who uses his or her power to punish, manipulate, or disparage a student beyond what would be considered a reasonable disciplinary procedure. I point out that the impact of teacher bullying can be more devastating and developmentally destructive than peer-on-peer bullying due to the importance of positive teacher–student relationships to a students' school success. I point out that teacher bullying is especially difficult to assess and address because teacher's bullying behaviors are often equated with maintaining order and discipline and, therefore, are "undetectable." In fact, current school policies do not even recognize teacher-to-student bullying as a problem and, consequently, fail to provide any formal mechanism to remedy student complaints against abusive teachers. I explore the few studies that have focused on this largely taboo topic within the bullying literature.

In Chapter 6, I discuss strategies that do not work in combating bullying and then describe the philosophy and key features of a whole-school approach as a framework for developing and implementing comprehensive bullying prevention and intervention strategies, including a detailed discussion of school-level, classroom-level, and student-level components. I also discuss a number of innovative programs and strategies that schools are currently using to combat bullying, including using shelter dogs. I point out that 47 states have passed antibullying legislation and all but six state laws contain prohibitions against cyberbullying. One of the most highly contentious issues is whether state antibullying laws should include provisions that specifically enumerate certain student populations (i.e., LGBT students and students with disabilities), who have been shown to be at greater risk of being victimized by bullies. I conclude this chapter by viewing bullying within a human rights framework. I argue that organizations such as schools have an obligation to uphold human rights standards, which include the right for a child to feel safe in school and to be spared the oppression and repeated, intentional humiliation.

The appendix contains a number of additional bullying resources. These resources include a compendium of assessment tools for measuring bullying victimization, perpetration, and bystander experiences; bullying prevention curricula and fact sheets; cyberbullying resources; and LGBT bullying resources.

My hope in writing this volume is that it will assist educators, parents, students, and other interested individuals to understand bullying in all its forms and complexity and to plan and implement comprehensive and effective interventions across a number of levels based on this complex understanding. My hope in writing this volume is that it will assist educators, parents, students, and other interested individuals to understand bullying in all its forms and complexity and to plan and implement comprehensive and effective interventions across a number of levels based on this complex understanding.

Acknowledgments

I greatly appreciate Autumn Lowry's time and assistance with this volume. I want to acknowledge her and thank her for writing the bullying vignettes contained in Box 2.1 of this volume as well as her help with indexing. I also want to thank Katrina Jordan for her excellent research on sexual bullying.

I especially want to acknowledge and thank my wife, Ann Contole, my partner of over 30 years, my confidante, my best friend, and my love. I thank her for her excellent editing skills as well as her ongoing encouragement and unending support throughout the years. I dedicate this volume to Ann and to our three daughters, Amy, Chrissy, and Laura. I thank each of you for bringing such joy into my life!

SCHOOL BULLYING

1

An Ecological-Systems Perspective of Bullying in Schools

> Love and compassion are necessities, not luxuries. Without them, humanity cannot survive.
>
> —*Dalai Lama XIV*

In order to combat bullying in our schools, it is essential that we broaden our focus. Research findings over the past several decades have enhanced our understanding of this complex phenomenon in important ways. For example, we have learned that bullying defies simple explanations and "silver-bullet" solutions. We have also learned that we must resist singling out the bully and the victim and broaden our focus to take into account a number of systemic factors that contribute to the bullying phenomenon "while not losing sight [sic] of the individual's contribution to a given behavior" (Center for Mental Health in Schools at UCLA, 2011, p. 7). These systemic factors include families, peer groups, teacher–student relationships, parent–child relationships, parent–school relationships, and cultural expectations. We also need to challenge several strongly held beliefs. Specifically, we need to challenge the belief that children and youth who bully are pathological and dysfunctional individuals who are in need of rehabilitation. Just as important, we need to challenge the strongly held belief that bullying victims need to learn how to fight off bullies by learning self-defense skills. These are misguided approaches to the bullying problem in schools. Instead, we need to view bullying as a transactional event in which no single factor provides an adequate understanding of this complex problem (Swearer, Espelage, Vaillancourt, & Hymel, 2010; Ungar, 2011). One of the major challenges facing educators, researchers, and the general public concerned about bullying in our schools and communities is to acknowledge its complexity and to develop and implement interventions that take into account all these various factors.

This chapter provides a rationale for and describes an ecological-systems perspective of bullying. It describes bullying within the larger culture, the mixed messages that children and youth receive about bullying from adults, the culture of bullying that exists in some schools, and the extent to which there may be a biological and developmental explanation for bullying behaviors.

An Ecological-Systems Perspective of Bullying

We have learned that a number of factors at multiple levels of the social environment contribute to and maintain bullying. The ecological-systems perspective is a very useful framework for increasing our understanding of bullying in all of its complexity as well as developing interventions based on this complex understanding. The ecological-systems framework is conceptualized as a "series of concentric circles of influence, which include intrapersonal, family, peer, community, and wider societal influences on behavior and development" (Banyard, Cross, & Modecki, 2006, p. 1315). Within this framework, each student is viewed as an inseparable part of the various social systems (e.g., school, home, neighborhood, peer group) within which he or she must function (Apter & Propper, 1986).

This ecological-systems perspective of bullying has begun to receive empirical support. For example, bullying is increasingly recognized as a group phenomenon that can be fully addressed only when one considers peer group processes (Vaillancourt, Hymel, & McDougall, 2003). A recent study by Barboza et al. (2009) found statistically significant effects between bullying and a number of environmental factors, including media effects, peer and family support systems, self-efficacy, and school environment. Based on their findings, these authors concluded that "our conceptual understanding of bullying behavior is advanced by using an ecological model as the theoretical lens . . . [b]ullying is a complex behavior with multiple causes and risk factors, ranging from individual characteristics to school settings to broader social contexts. In our view, the ecological perspective provides both a vehicle for better understanding the complex features of bullying and also for crafting sensitive and effective interventions at multiple contextual levels" (pp. 116 & 119).

Our examination of bullying utilizing an ecological-systems perspective begins at the broadest possible level—our culture. We live in a conflict-filled, competitive world where bullying is pervasive. Bullying behavior is evident in our international relationships, work environments, politics, sports, media, and even in our homes.

Bullying in Our Schools Is a Reflection of Bullying in Our Culture

What do we see when we observe the behavior of adults in our society who serve as role models for our youth? What do kids learn about interpersonal relationships and resolving conflicts by watching adults? Bullying behavior pervades our culture. For example, we see bullying at the international level when powerful countries impose their will on less powerful countries through economic, political, or military force (Parsons, 2005). In the political arena, we see politicians who attempt to "embarrass, humiliate, and expose one's political enemies as fools and incompetents..." (Rigby, 2002, p. 97). In football and other competitive sports, we see older players bullying and harassing younger players, and we witness parents losing control and screaming insults at the referees. We hear role models such as tennis player Venus Williams say, "I think if you have the opportunity to bully your opponent, then you have to take that chance. If you have the power, it's perfect to use it" (Rigby, 2002, p. 96). In our workplaces, we hear about aggressive adults who bully their subordinates (Salin, 2003).

The media must also be examined for the messages and behaviors it communicates to its youthful viewers. A disproportionate percentage of preteens, adolescents, and young adults watch popular reality shows such as *Jersey Shore* and *Real Housewives* where competition, scheming, humiliation, backbiting, betrayal, and callousness are presented as "ways to get ahead" (Christenson & Ivancin, 2006). The reality show *The Biggest Loser* routinely humiliates overweight participants by having them wear skimpy clothing during public weigh-ins (Christenson & Ivancin, 2006). A 2010 Kaiser Family Foundation survey found that American children and teens spend an average of 7 hours a day engaged with a variety of "entertainment screens"—television, cell phones, handheld games, iPads, Internet games, Facebook, and video games, with 2 hours or more being spent playing violent video games (Benson, 2011). Some researchers have shown a correlation between aggressive behavior and the viewing of violent video games. Of particular concern is the development of a computer video game by Rockstar Games (publishers of the Grand Theft Auto games) called "Bully," released in October 2006, "where players adopt the persona of a 15-year-old juvenile delinquent who terrorizes his victims with a range of physically and psychologically abusive behaviors" (Barboza et al., 2009, p. 105).

We must also examine and acknowledge the bullying behaviors that occur in varied forms in many of our homes. While we do not characterize spouse abuse, child abuse, and domestic violence as bullying (Rigby, 2002), these aggressive and violent acts involve the basic characteristic of bullying behaviors, namely, the *systematic abuse of power*. It could be persuasively argued that our culture has "institutionalized bullying...which no doubt dramatically affects our children, through poor adult role models..." (Twemlow & Sacco, 2007, p. 245). Why should we be surprised that we have a bullying problem in our schools?

Mixed Messages About Bullying Behavior

To compound the problem, our youth are also receiving mixed and confusing messages about bullying behavior from adults. Adults' actions often do not match their words and arbitrarily justify certain behaviors. Parsons (2005) describes how these mixed messages and blurred lines can confuse our children and youth and complicate our efforts to combat bullying:

> As we begin to pit one student's achievements and abilities against another's—in sports, school, or the arts—the line between competitiveness and aggressiveness becomes blurred. Competitive individuals strive to prove themselves superior to others while respecting the goals and rights of others: aggressive individuals strive to prove themselves superior to others by subjugating them through an unfair or irrational use of power. That's a sophisticated distinction that many adults, let alone young people, have a hard time making. Children [and youth] become critically confused, however, when they start to qualify the principle that all people are created equal by adding that some people are created more equal than others. Therein lies the justification for bullies to aggress against others...once children [and youth] start to believe that all people are created equal except for people of a certain skin color, or a particular religion, or possessing a physical or mental disability, then Pandora's Box is broken wide open. The concept of exclusion is sanctioned (Parsons, 2005, p.79).

As much as adults talk about proper behavior and morals, our children and youth continue to learn the most from observing the actions of adults (Hsiao-chuan, 2011). Their observations of adults lead to a number of troubling questions: "When should students cooperate and when should they compete?," "What's wrong with putting people down, finding an edge to use to one's advantage, or making a distinction between 'us' and 'them' when everybody does it, even teachers"? In the eyes of a student bully, "aggression is rationalized as strength, competitiveness as license to prey on others, and bigotry as proof of status" (Parsons, 2005, p. 85). In the end, adults should not blame children for behaviors that result from observing and modeling adult behavior. Which brings us to the question: Is there a culture of bullying in some schools, and how might this bullying culture impact peer-on-peer bullying?

A Bullying School Culture?

We know that a school's culture and climate significantly affect and influence students' behavior and learning (Wang, Haertel, & Walberg, 1997). A school's culture has been defined as "the beliefs and expectations apparent in a school's daily routine, including *how colleagues interact with each other...*" (Hamilton & Richardson, 1995, p. 369). A school's climate has been described as "the heart and soul of a school. It is about that essence of a school that leads a child, a teacher, an administrator, a staff member to look forward to each school day..." (Freiberg & Stein, 1999). How do a school's culture and climate impact bullying behaviors? A positive school climate, where students and teachers could be trusted, students were treated with respect, and rules were perceived to be fair, has been found to be associated with fewer reports of bullying and victimization (Guerra, Williams, & Sadek, 2011). It has also been shown that a positive and supportive school climate was associated with more help-seeking attitudes among students (Eliot, Cornell, Gregory, & Fan, 2010).

Unfortunately, a culture of bullying exists in some schools. As Parsons (2005) states, "bullying hinges on a power imbalance. Principals wield the same uncomfortable power over everyone in their schools as teachers wield in their classrooms. In effective schools, principals ignore the allure of power and strive to empower others to keep finding solutions to the thorniest of problems, including bullying. In bullying schools, the principal is often the source of the problem" (p. 65). In bullying schools, bullying behavior pervades relationships at a number of levels. Adults in schools with "bullying cultures" help to normalize bullying because they continually model bullying behaviors themselves (Viadero, 2010). Besides principals bullying teachers, office staff, students, and parents, we have teachers who bully other teachers, students, and parents, and we have parents who bully teachers, office staff, principals, and even their own children (Parsons, 2005). To combat bullying in schools, we must first acknowledge its existence in all its forms in our schools (Parsons, 2005).

Is Bullying Part of Our Human Nature?

Why is bullying behavior so rampant throughout our culture? We end this chapter by exploring the extent to which there may be a biological explanation for bullying behavior. Any notion that human beings lived in harmony with each other at any time in history is a myth (Vaughn & Santos, 2007). Evolutionary biologists contend that "striving for social dominance is part of human nature" (Rigby, 2002, p. 151) and that the roots of bullying "lie in the group behavior of our species that singles out a scapegoat to victimize and abuse" (Underwood, Rish-Scott, & Springer, 2011, p. 11). The potential for victimization and scapegoating is exacerbated by the physiological and psychological changes that mark early adolescence. Early adolescence is the life stage marked by puberty as well as the stage where social status and peer affiliation become important (Nishina, 2004). Much more time is spent with peers, and much less time is spent with family members (Nishina, 2004). A peer-based theory that is frequently mentioned in the bullying literature is the homophily hypothesis, which states that "aggressive youths affiliate with other aggressive youths" and that this peer group affiliation results in bullying behaviors (Swearer et al., 2010, p. 39). Consequently, it is important to understand bullying within the context of peer group affiliation. It is also important to understand the importance of students who witness bullying since their behaviors and reactions (e.g., laughter and taunting) can encourage and even prolong bullying incidents (Swearer et al., 2010). It should not surprise us that these dramatic physiological and social changes, combined with the move from elementary to middle school (with less structure and a decrease in adult supervision), result in a spike in bullying behaviors in 6th grade followed by a steady decline in later grades (Nishina, 2004). The importance of the peer group in understanding and combating bullying is discussed in greater detail in Chapter 2 of this volume.

Summary

Bullying is a complex phenomenon that defies simple explanations and simple solutions. The ecological-systems perspective is a very useful framework for increasing our understanding of bullying in all of its complexity as well as developing interventions based on this complex understanding. This ecological-systems perspective of bullying has begun to receive empirical support.

Bullying in our schools is a reflection of bullying in our culture. We live in a conflict-filled, competitive world where bullying is pervasive. Bullying behavior is evident in our international relationships, work environments, politics, sports, media, and even in our homes. To compound the problem, our youth are also receiving mixed messages from adults about bullying behavior. In the end, adults should not blame children for behaviors that result from observing and modeling adult behavior. We know that a school's culture and climate significantly affect and influence students' behavior. Unfortunately, a culture of bullying exists in some schools that serves to normalize bullying within that school.

According to evolutionary biologists, striving for social dominance is part of human nature. The potential for victimization and scapegoating are exacerbated by the physiological and psychological changes that mark early adolescence. This includes the increasing importance of social status and peer group affiliation and explains a spike in bullying behaviors in 6th grade followed by a steady decline in later grades.

2

■ ■ ■

What Do We Know About Face-to-Face Peer Bullying?

> The greatness of humanity is not in being human, but in being humane.
>
> —*Mahatma Gandhi*

This chapter presents a brief history of research on face-to-face peer bullying, provides a definition of bullying that is used throughout this volume, and differentiates bullying from other types of peer conflict. It discusses factors that contribute to bullying across a number of contexts including individual characteristics, family characteristics, and school characteristics. It presents recent statistics on the extent of and types of face-to-face bullying in schools and discusses which children and youth are at greatest risk of becoming victims of bullying. It discusses the educational and emotional consequences for victims, the bullies themselves, as well as those who are both bullies and victims (i.e., "bully-victims"). This chapter concludes with a discussion of several important developments in recent research on bullying that challenge some commonly held perceptions: the socially connected, popular bully; the critical role of peers who witness bullying; and the ways in which teachers and other adults in school perceive and respond to bullying incidents.

A Brief History of Research on Bullying

Systematic research on bullying in the United States is a relatively recent development. For example, it was not until the late 1980s and early 1990s that bullying began to attract attention in the United States (Olweus & Limber, 2010). Since that time, research on this topic has grown tremendously. In the mid-2000s, there was a marked shift in bullying research toward research on cyberbullying (Smith, 2011). (A detailed discussion of cyberbullying can be found in Chapter 3 of this volume.) Similarly, state laws that focused on combating bullying in schools were nonexistent in 1999 (Olweus & Limber, 2010). However, as of early 2012, all but three states in the United States have passed some form of antibullying legislation (American Foundation for Suicide Prevention, 2011). (A more detailed discussion of antibullying laws across the United States can be found in Chapter 6 of this volume).

What Is Bullying?

Based on my extensive research on this topic, I believe that the most succinct and useful way of conceptualizing bullying in all of its forms is as a "a systematic abuse of power" (Rigby, 2002). This "systematic abuse of power" differentiates bullying from other forms of aggression and conflict, and as such, I discuss bullying from this perspective throughout this volume.

Beyond the general notion of defining bullying as a systematic abuse of power, a number of researchers have focused on three key elements in definitions of bullying. Specifically, bullying refers to the *unprovoked* physical or psychological abuse of an individual by one student or a group of students *over time* to create an *ongoing pattern of abuse* against a victim *who cannot easily defend him or herself.* In other words, bullying is a specific type of aggression that involves an imbalance of power where the bully consciously intends to harm his or her victim physically and/or psychologically and has the power and the means to do so. Youth who engage in bullying behaviors have a need to feel powerful and in control, and they derive satisfaction from inflicting injury/suffering on their victims (Center for School Mental Health Assistance, 2002). Bullies are also skilled at "picking victims who are unlikely to fight back and for finding victims in unsupervised settings where they can't walk away or find an adult to help" (Goodwin, 2011, p. 83). The public tears of victims often serve to solidify the power and status of the bully (Jacobson, 2010). Table 2.1 contains a listing of the various forms of bullying and respective definitions, and Box 2.1 contains examples of several common forms of bullying.

Table 2.1 Types of Bullying

Term	Definition
Physical bullying	An attack on a victim that is physical in nature, including hitting, kicking, pushing, poking, hair pulling, excessive tickling, punching, choking, taking or damaging belongings
Verbal bullying	Includes such acts as calling hurtful names, taunting, threatening, malicious teasing
Relational/Indirect bullying	A form of bullying where the bully does not directly confront the victim but covertly attempts to socially isolate and exclude the victim from social groups and social events. It includes the spreading of vicious rumors intended to damage one's reputation, rejecting and humiliating the victim, and manipulating friendships.
Cyberbullying (see chapter 3 of this volume)	Cyberbullying has been defined as the repeated use of computers, cell phones, and other electronic devices to harm, harass, humiliate, threaten, or damage the reputation and relationships of the intended victim. It includes "sexting," which is the act of sending sexually explicit messages or photographs, primarily between mobile phones. It involves "private (such as chat or text messaging), semi-public (such as posting a harassing message on an email list), or public communications (such as creating a website devoted to making fun of the victim)" (Schrock & Boyd, 2011, p. 374).
Sexual bullying	Any physical or verbal bullying behavior that is based on a person's sexuality or gender. It includes making fun of someone for being homosexual, making fun of the size of a girl's breasts or buttocks, using sexual terms (e.g., "slut," "bitch") to put someone down, making jokes about rape, spreading rumors about someone's sex life, touching parts of someone's body where they don't want to be touched, and putting pressure on someone to act in a sexual manner (e.g., sexual propositioning). It also includes exhibitionism.
Bias bullying	Bullying that is based on (or justified by) the victim being a member of a particular group, often a marginalized or disadvantaged one, rather than on individual characteristics

Note. *Sources:* Center for Mental Health in Schools at UCLA, 2011; Crick et al., 2001; Espelage, 2004; Hinduja & Patchin, 2007; Holladay, 2010; Ragozzino and O'Brien, 2009; Schrock & Boyd, 2011.

Box 2.1 Examples of Several Common Forms of Bullying

Physical Bullying

Brandon, a student at Valley Middle School, just got a new jacket for his birthday. When he wears it to school, Kyle, another student, begins to taunt Brandon about his jacket. When Brandon asks Kyle to stop, Kyle laughs at him and pushes him up against the lockers. Brandon tries to push away from Kyle, but the more Brandon tries, the harder Kyle pushes. Finally, Kyle kicks Brandon, and as Brandon falls, Kyle takes Brandon's jacket from him and stomps it then spits on it.

Verbal Bullying

Kate is a freshman at East High School and is nervous about her first day of high school. Everything appears to go smoothly until it is time for gym class. As Kate comes out of the locker room, she hears the other girls laughing and saying things like "She can barely even fit into her gym clothes!" Kate tries to ignore them, but when it is time for warm-up laps around the gym track, she can hear them laughing again and saying things such as "Look how red her face is! The fatso can't even handle warm-ups!" Another girl points and laughs and says, "Look at her, she looks like a waddling duck when she runs because she's so fat!" Kate can't bear to listen anymore and runs into the bathroom crying.

Relational/Indirect Bullying

Rachel and Christine are both students at Hartford High School. Rachel does not like Christine because she feels that everyone likes Christine more than they like her. Rachel begins a rumor about Christine in science class, saying that she has been "hooking up with every guy on the football team." Before lunchtime, many students hear the rumor and distort it even further. By the end of the day, several students begin to ask Christine how she likes "being so easy." Over the next few weeks, Christine begins to feel the effects of the rumor worsen. She loses her student council election, her cheerleading coach speaks to her about "the reputation of the squad," and her boyfriend breaks up with her because he thinks she cheated on him. Christine doesn't know where the rumor started or how she will ever rebuild her reputation.

Cyberbullying

Dean is a student at King Middle School who just tried out for the football team. As he comes off of the field after doing poorly on his throwing and running, he feels pretty discouraged. He can even hear the older players laughing at him, but he doesn't look up at them to see who they are. Certain he isn't going to make the team after such an awful tryout, Dean just wants to go home. After having dinner with his parents, Dean logs online to check his social network sites. To his horrific surprise, cell phone videos of Dean's embarrassing try-out have been uploaded and posted all over many students' social network sites. There are multiple comments making fun of Dean's performance by dozens of students. Just when Dean thinks it can't get worse, he gets a text message from one of his friends asking if he knows about the pictures and videos being texted and sent via cell phone. Dean is sure by the next day that the whole school will access to the video and picture proof of his bad tryout. He doesn't want to go to school to find out.

Sexual Bullying

Bailey is a student at West High School who has been having trouble with another student, Allan. Allan has been sexually proposition-ing Bailey for a few weeks. He stops her in the hallway, talks to her in class, and sends her texts about how "hot" she is and states how badly he "wants her" and how they should "hook up." Sometimes when they pass in the hall, he even makes illicit remarks about her body in front of other students. Bailey is not only frustrated but also getting uneasy with Allan's persistence after telling him "no" several times and asking him to stop. Allan's unrelenting behavior only worsens. He begins to touch Bailey's hair in class and tries to whisper sexually explicit phrases in her ear from the desk behind her. One day when class lets out and the halls become crowded, Allan runs his hand across Bailey's breast and squeezes. Bailey slaps Allan's hand away and runs to the principal's office to report Allan's behavior.

Bias Bullying

Joseph is a 6th grade Latino student at Marsden Middle School who lives alone with his mother. His mother is a waitress who works almost every day and picks up double shifts several times a week to be able to pay the household bills and have a little left over for Joseph's lunch money. Most students at school know that Joseph and his mom do not have a lot of money. Almost daily, Joseph hears other kids at school taunt and ridicule him about being poor, saying things like "nasty Mexican," "so poor and ugly his Dad couldn't even love him enough to stick around," and several other hurtful things. Joseph cannot understand why the other students are mean to him and begins to skip school when his mom is at work.

I have referred to bullying as a low-level form of violence in schools (Dupper & Meyer-Adams, 2002). This is because bullying in schools is largely "hidden" from adults and is more insidious than high-level violence. Much more attention needs to be focused on low-level violence in schools, such as bullying, since low-level violence can impact its victims in substantial ways (Boxer, Edwards-Leeper, Goldstein, Musher-Eizenman, & Dubow, 2003) as well as escalate into more serious acts of violence (Goldstein, 1999). I view peer-on-peer bullying as *peer child abuse*. As such, victims of peer bullying are no different from victims of child abuse. Just as we do not expect child abuse victims to "fight off" their abusers, we should not expect bullying victims to "fight off" bullies on their own. Peer bullies should be confronted and held accountable for their actions, and victims of bullying need the help and support of peers and adults in order to stop the bullying.

How Is Bullying Different From Other Types of Peer Conflict?

It is important to be able to distinguish between bullying and other types of peer conflict. While any two people of relatively equal status can have a conflict or a disagreement or even a fight, as stated earlier, bullying only occurs where there is a power imbalance with the victim having a difficult time defending him or herself (U.S. Department of Health and Human Services, n.d.,e).

Since teasing is a "rite of passage" and a hallmark of male-to-male adolescent friendship (Darling, 2010), it is extremely important to differentiate teasing from bullying. While some teasing and exchanging of insults can become relatively aggressive in nature, teasing is not intended to harm the other person (Doll, Song, Champion, & Jones, 2011). While a bully fully intends to harm his or her victim from the outset, a "teaser" seeks to elicit some type of reaction from the other person initially. How the other person reacts to a teasing episode will largely determine how the interaction proceeds. For example, if a boy laughs off a comment about his pants being too short, the teasing episode may stop right there. However, if the boy reacts angrily after hearing that his pants are too short, the interaction might evolve into a fight among peers of equal status. Or the "teaser" may decide to intentionally harm his victim on a chronic basis, and the initial teasing episode evolves into bullying (Darling, 2010).

Factors Associated With Bullying at Various Contextual Levels

As stated in Chapter 1 of this volume, bullying is a complex behavior with multiple causes and risk factors (Barboza et al., 2009). Research findings by Barboza et al. and others have increased our understanding of specific factors that contribute to bullying across a number of contexts, including individual characteristics (see Table 2.2), family characteristics (see Table 2.3), and a number of school characteristics (see Table 2.4). As seen in Table 2.2, one's temperament is the best-documented individual characteristic associated with bullying behaviors. It also appears that being impulsive, easily frustrated, and having lower-levels of empathy are associated with bullying behaviors. There is also growing evidence that bullies, rather than feeling bad about themselves, have average to above-average self-esteem and that bullies are often more confident and socially astute than generally assumed (Kazdin & Rotella, 2009). We can also see in Table 2.2 that males are more likely to be bullies than females and that males engage in direct (i.e., physical and verbal attacks) bullying as opposed to females, who engage more frequently in indirect (i.e., spreading rumors, manipulation) bullying.

Table 2.3 identifies a number of family characteristics that have been found to be associated with being a bully. A significant predictor of engaging in bullying behaviors is coming from a home where a child has experienced physical and/or emotional abuse and where there is aggression among siblings. The role of the father in the family also appears to be important. For example, coming from a family where a father is a bully himself or where a father is

Table 2.2 Individual Characteristics Associated With Children and Youth Who Engage in Bullying Behaviors

Temperament	The best-documented individual factor in bullying is temperament. Students who are active and impulsive in temperament may be more inclined to develop into bullies. Students who bully their peers regularly tend to be easily frustrated, have low levels of empathy, have difficulty following rules, view violence positively, are defiant toward adults, break school rules, have poorer school adjustment, and are more likely to drink alcohol and smoke. Male bullies tend to be physically stronger than other children.
Having good self-esteem	Most research indicates that children and youth who bully have average or above average self-esteem. Scant evidence exists to support the contention that bullies victimize others because they feel bad about themselves.
Being a bullying victim	Victims of bullying are more likely to bully others, and the odds of bullying increase significantly with age.
Being male	Males consistently exhibit a higher probability of bullying than females. Boys are much more likely to report being bullies, and boys are more likely to be the perpetrators of "direct" bullying (bullying that involves direct physical or verbal attacks). Girls are more likely to use "indirect" bullying (social exclusion, manipulation of friendship relationships, spreading rumors).

Note. *Sources:* Barboza et al., 2009; Center for School Mental Health Assistance, 2002; Haynie et al., 2001; U.S. Department of Health and Human Services, n.d.,d; Vaillancourt, Hymel, & McDougall, 2003.

absent is associated with children who are bullies. It also appears that family relationships that lack warmth as well as families with inconsistent parental discipline are associated with children and youth who bully others.

Table 2.4 identifies a number of school characteristics that have been shown to be associated with bullying. This is an important area of current and future research on bullying since it takes into account factors in the larger environment that can serve to reinforce or diminish the likelihood of bullying in a particular school. Research has indicated that a negative

Table 2.3 Family Characteristics and Dynamics Associated With Youth
Who Engage in Bullying Behaviors

Aggressive behavior and violence are common in the family	Bullies often come from homes where physical punishment is used. This modeling of aggressive behavior at home toward the child by parents or by parents toward each other is associated with bullying. Sibling aggression and abuse are also significant predictors of bullying involvement. A high level of sibling violence is often found in the homes of bully-victims, with the majority of bully-victims admitting that they both bully and are victimized by their siblings. There is also an association between being physically or emotionally abused as a child and engaging in bullying behavior.
Having a father who is a bully or an absent father	Fathers who were bullies in school are more likely to have sons who bully others. Bullies are also likely to grow up in homes without a father figure and/ or where mothers are perceived to be relatively powerless.
Inconsistent discipline	Children who engage in bullying are more likely to come from homes in which parents are overly permissive and do not set limits on or monitor their children's behavior.
Lacking warmth and closeness	Families of bullies are also characterized as lacking warmth and lacking close relationships.

Note. *Sources:* Center for School Mental Health Assistance, 2002; Duncan, 2011; Farrington, 1993; Ragozzino & O'Brien, 2009; Smith, 2011.

school climate, poor teacher–student relationships, low levels of adult supervision, and the absence of school security procedures or devices are all associated with higher levels of reported bullying in schools.

How Extensive Is Bullying in Schools?

Bullying at school has been on the rise since 2001 (DeVoe, Kaffenberger, & Chandler, 2005) and appears to be widespread in our public schools today. Estimates of bullying differ depending on whether it is measured on a daily, weekly, or monthly basis as well as the grade level where it occurs. According to recent national survey data on school violence and student safety from the National Center for Education Statistics (NCES) as well

Table 2.4 School Characteristics Associated With Bullying

Student perceptions of school climate	A school climate characterized as unpleasant, unfair, and unwelcoming by students increases the probability of bullying. Bullying is more prevalent in school environments where students receive negative feedback and negative attention on a regular basis.
Teacher–student relationships	Having poor relationships with teachers is associated with more bullying while perceived social support from teachers has been shown to be associated with lower levels of bullying.
Structure and adult supervision	Low levels of adult supervision in the school playground, school yard, and hallways are associated with higher levels of bullying. Less school structure has also been shown to be associated with higher levels of bullying.
School security procedures or devices	Students were less likely to report being bullied in schools with target-hardening devices or procedures (e.g., metal detectors, security cameras) and/or campus police officers.
Attitudes of school personnel toward bullying	There is less bullying in schools where school personnel adopt antibullying values and actively intervene during bullying episodes. Conversely, there is a higher probability of bullying in schools where school personnel tolerate, ignore, or dismiss bullying behaviors.

Note. *Sources:* Center for School Mental Health Assistance, 2002; Cohn & Canter, 2003; DeVoe, Kaffenberger, & Chandler, 2005; Doll, Song, Champion & Jones, 2011; Espelage, 2004; Swearer, Espelage, Vaillancourt, & Hymel, 2010; Troop-Gordon & Kopp, 2011.

as data from the 2009–2010 School Survey on Crime and Safety, a much higher percentage of middle schools (39%) reported bullying on a daily or weekly basis compared with high schools (20%) or elementary schools (20%) (Neiman, 2011). These findings are comparable to other nationally representative surveys of high school–age students, which indicate that over a 12-month period as many as 20 percent of students experience bullying on school property (CDC, 2011). A recent national survey involving over 43,000 students found that half of U.S. high school students admitted to bullying someone in the past year, and 47% reported being bullied, teased, or taunted "in a way that seriously upset them" in the past year (Josephson Institute, 2010). Other studies have reported that 61% of girls and 60% of boys had been bullied one or more times a month (Nishioka Coe, Burke, Hanita, & Sprague, 2011) and that 7% of students face bullying *every day* (Center for Mental Health in Schools at UCLA, 2011).

Based on these findings, it appears that bullying occurs at all school levels, including preschool, with more direct physical forms of bullying escalating through elementary school and middle school and gradually declining as students reach high school. Verbal bullying appears to increase as students move into middle and high school (Institute of Education Sciences, 2011). Bullying occurs in rural, suburban, and urban schools, and among children of every income level, race, and geographic region (U.S. Department of Health and Human Services, n.d.,e). Bullying occurs most frequently in school hallways or stairwells (47.2%) and classrooms (33.6%) (Institute of Education Sciences, 2011), with the notable exception of cyberbullying (see Chapter 3 of this volume for a detailed discussion of cyberbullying).

It is also important to note that these bullying statistics may seriously underestimate the true extent of bullying in schools. There are several reasons for this. First, students may not report being a victim of bullying because it would require the victim to acknowledge him or herself as powerless as well as require the perpetrator to acknowledge him or herself as abusive (Boyd & Marwick, 2011). Second, victims of bullying may be reluctant to report their victimization out of concern that nothing will be done about it and that their "tattling" will result in more severe bullying incidents in the future (Franks, 2010).

What Types of Bullying Occur in Schools?

It appears that the majority of bullying incidents are verbal (54%) or relational (51%) in nature, including such behaviors as spreading rumors or ostracizing the victim; fewer than 30% of bullying incidents are physical in nature (Goodwin, 2011; Petrosino, Guckenburg, DeVoe, & Hanson, 2010; Wang Iannotti, & Nansel, 2009). According to the most recent NCES national survey, 21% of respondents reported that they had been made fun of by their peers, 18% reported that they had been the subject of rumors, 11% reported that they had been pushed, shoved, tripped, or spit on, and 6% reported that they had been threatened with harm (Robers, Zhang, & Truman, 2010).

Which Groups of Children/Youth Are at Greatest Risk of Becoming Victims of Bullies?

The most reliable predictor of becoming a bullying victim is being viewed as "not fitting in" or "being different" in some way (Furlong, Chung,

Bates, & Morrison, 1995; Shakeshift et al., 1995). For example, girls who are perceived by their peers as physically unattractive or physically well developed, or who do not dress stylishly, are often victims of bullying. Other victims of bullying include students who are known to be or presumed to be gay or lesbian, including boys who do not fit a stereotypic macho male image (see Chapter 4 of this volume for a detailed discussion of LGBT bullying). Other students who are at risk of becoming bullying victims include students who have a religion that is different from the majority (see Chapter 5 of this volume for a detailed discussion of religious bullying), students who wear unique and unusual clothing, and students who exhibit physical or emotional weaknesses (Furlong et al., 1995; Shakeshift et al., 1995). In addition, overweight and obese students are often victims of bullying (Janssen, Craig, Boyce, & Pickett, 2004; Lumeng et al., 2010). Students with disabilities (e.g., LD [learning disability], ADHD [attention deficit hyperactivity disorder]) are two to three times more at risk of being bullied as well as at greater risk of taking part in bullying others (Knox & Conti-Ramsden, 2003; U.S. Department of Health and Human Services, n.d.,c). Children with medical conditions that affect their appearance (e.g., cerebral palsy, muscular dystrophy, and spinal bifida) (Dawkins, 1996) and children who have diabetes and who are dependent on insulin (U.S. Department of Health and Human Services, n.d.,c) are also at higher risk of being bullied at school.

Victims of bullying also share some personal characteristics, in general. For example, victims are typically quiet, shy, anxious, insecure, and cautious; have few friends; are socially isolated; and rarely defend themselves or retaliate when confronted by students who bully them (Cohn & Canter, 2003). Victims of bullying often have overprotective parents and overly close relationships with siblings (Cohn & Canter, 2003; Duncan, 2011).

What Are the Educational and Emotional Consequences for Victims of Chronic Bullying?

Bullying is no longer viewed as a normative phase that most children outgrow, but rather, bullying is now linked to a broad range of long-term harmful effects (Nansel et al., 2001). There is substantial evidence, based on the findings of longitudinal studies across four continents, that being a victim of bullying "is consistently associated with depression, loneliness, social anxiety, school phobia, and low self-esteem" (Greene, 2006, p. 71). Victimized youth are also at increased risk for mental health problems such as depression and anxiety, and psychosomatic complaints such as headaches and poor school adjustment (Smokowski & Kopasz, 2005). Victims of bullying have higher rates of eating disorders, lower academic achievement and school connectedness, and higher rates of truancy and disciplinary problems (Craig, 1998; Gastic, 2008; Gini, 2008; Kaltiala-Heino, Rimpela, Rantanen, & Rimpela, 2000; O'Brennan, Bradshaw, & Sawyer, 2009; You et al., 2008).

Recent neuroscience research findings provide additional evidence that the short- and long-term impact of psychological forms of bullying can be as devastating for the victim as physical abuse. Specifically, it has been discovered that psychological forms of bullying activate the same regions of the brain as physical pain and that bullying can, over time, alter brain functioning in ways that increase a victim's "sensitivity to future victimization and pain...[and] jeopardize [one's] capacity for effective functioning" (Vaillancourt, Hymel & McDougell, 2011, p. 29-30).

Youth who are bullied have also been shown to be at greater risk of developing poor self-esteem, depression, and suicidal ideations, and at greater risk of attempting suicide (Ivarsson, Broberg, Arvidsson, & Gillberg, 2005; Klomek, Marracco, Kleinman, Schonfeld, & Gould, 2007; Patchin & Hinduja, 2010; Roland, 2002). Among middle school students, bullying victims were 3 times, and bully-victims were 6.6 times more likely to report seriously considering suicide compared with youth who were not victims of bullies (Centers for Disease Control and Prevention, 2011). However, the small number of studies that have focused on the link between bullying and suicide have shown that youth who complete suicide after being bullied had other serious suicide risk factors including mental health or substance abuse problems, a family history of suicide, or a previous suicide attempt (Underwood et al., 2011). As a result, Underwood et al. (2011) emphasize the importance of being "alert to preexisting suicide risk factors when dealing with a youth who may be a victim of bullying" (p. 13).

There is also evidence that there is potential for escalating violence resulting from bullying incidents. According to a recent national report, 4.1% of bullied students ages 12 through 18 reported bringing a gun, knife, or other object that could be used as a weapon to school, compared with 2.1% students who were not bullied (Institute of Education Sciences, 2011). Table 2.5 summarizes the latest research findings on the educational and emotional consequences experienced by victims of bullying.

Table 2.5 The Educational and Emotional Consequences Experienced by Victims of Chronic Bullying

Victims of Chronic Bullying Are More Likely Than Other Students to:
Consider school to be an unsafe and unhappy place. It has been estimated that as many as 7% of America's 8th graders stay home at least once a month because of bullies
Have low social status (in contrast to bullies, who are often considered popular) reflecting the differential power status between bullies and their victims
Fear using the school bathroom
Fear riding on the school bus
Have poorer grades and increased rates of truancy and dropping out
Start fights or bring weapons to school to exact vengeance on the bully(ies)
Be depressed, lonely, anxious, have poor self-esteem, and think about suicide
Have psychosomatic problems (e.g., headaches, sleep disturbances)
Develop even more severe mental health problems such as psychotic symptoms

Note. *Sources:* Center for School Mental Health Assistance, 2002; Hazler, 1994; Juvonen & Graham, 2004; Limber, 2002; Olweus & Limber, 2010.

What Are the Educational and Emotional Consequences for the Bullies Themselves?

Youth who bully others are at increased risk for substance use, academic problems, and violence later in adolescence and adulthood (Smokowski & Kopasz, 2005). There is also evidence that bullying behavior in school predicts later criminality and delinquency (Hymel, Rocke-Henderson, & Bonanno, 2005). For example, bullies are five times more likely than their classmates to wind up in juvenile court, to be convicted of crimes, and, when they become adults, to have children with aggression problems (Hazler, 1994). Sixty percent of boys who were bullies in middle school and high school were convicted of one or more crimes before they reached the age of 25 while 40% had three or more convictions (Fox, Elliot, Kerlikowske, Newman, & Christenson, 2003). It has been reported that youth who bully their peers are more likely to report that they own guns to gain the respect of others or to frighten others (Cunningham, Henggeler, Limber, Melton, & Nation, 2000). In the most extreme cases, bullying has been linked to school shootings (Meyer-Adams & Conner, 2008). Youth who bully are also more likely to engage in bullying behavior in the workplace or in their future relationships with their partners (Garbarino & deLara, 2003). Interestingly, bullies were 4.1 times more likely to report seriously considering suicide compared with youth who were neither bullies nor victims (Underwood, Rish-Scott, & Springer, 2011).

What Are the Educational and Emotional Consequences for Bully-Victims?

A growing body of evidence suggests that, although they are a relatively small subset of students, bully-victims (i.e., children and youth who are bullied and who then go on to bully other youth) appear to be the most maladjusted group of students and the most likely group of students to remain chronically involved in bullying years later (Hamburger, Basile, & Vivolo, 2011; Nishina, 2004; O'Brennan, Bradshaw, & Sawyer, 2009). Specifically, one study found that bully-victims felt less safe and more disconnected to their school environments than their peers and were at increased risk for aggressive-impulsive behavior (O'Brennan, Bradshaw, & Sawyer, 2009). Compared with youth who only bully, or who are only victims, bully-victims suffer the most serious consequences and are at greater risk for both mental health and behavior problems (Smokowski & Kopasz, 2005). Of particular concern is the finding that bully-victims were 6.6 times more likely to report seriously considering suicide compared with youth who were neither bullied nor victims (Underwood, Rish-Scott, & Springer, 2011).

Socially Connected, Popular Bullies

As stated in Chapter 1 of this volume, we have recently begun to acknowledge the impact and importance of peer group dynamics on bullying. These recent findings are challenging some popular notions about bullies. Rather than view bullies as misfits, we are beginning to acknowledge that many school bullies have a wide variety of friends and are popular among their peers as a result of their physical attractiveness, athleticism, and highly developed social skills (Farmer et al., 2010). One example of a highly developed social skill is the way that a bully plans and anticipates the reaction of his or her victim and proceeds in a way that escapes adult detection (Coivin, Tobin, Beard, Hadan, & Sprague, 1998).

The high social status of many bullies further magnifies their power relative to the low social status of their victims (Juvonen & Graham, 2004). As a result, "popular" bullies are proactive and goal directed in their aggression (Farmer et al., 2010) Rodkin, 2011; Vaillancourt, McDougall, Hymel, & Sunderani, 2010). There are several types of "popularity" among bullies. One type is "perceived popularity" or how socially prominent the individuals are, and the other type is "sociometric popularity" or how well liked they are (Paul, 2011). Perceived popularity has been linked to high levels of "relational aggression" where efforts are made to socially isolate and exclude victims from social groups and social events (Hamburger et al., 2011). It appears that the capacity for aggression increases as peer status increases and that "aggression wanes only at the highest echelons of status, where its utility is questionable" (Faris & Felmlee, 2011, p. 49). Socially connected, popular students often bully students of the same sex "as part of a struggle for dominance, particularly in the beginning of the school year or between transitions from one school to another, when the social hierarchy is in flux and when unpopular children can be targeted" (Rodkin, 2011, p. 13). Some children may even bully peers in an effort to "fit in," even though they may be uncomfortable with the behavior (Cohn & Canter, 2003). It appears that many students "climb the social pyramid on the backs of other students, using ostracism, ridicule, and gossip to gain social status" (Goodwin, 2011).

Faris & Felmlee (2011) point out the importance of the social context of aggression and the link between status and violence by concluding:

> Our findings call into question several traditional assumptions, including the argument that isolated individuals on a group's fringes are the most likely to behave aggressively. Instead, aggression remains most common among centrally located students, with the exception of the few at the very top of the hierarchy. Moreover, we find that social factors at the dyad, group, and school level all powerfully shape harmful behavior in a school setting; these factors include the aggressive behavior of an adolescent's friends, location in the friendship hierarchy, and patterns of relationships between the genders in a school. (pp. 68–69)

These are noteworthy findings with important implications for combating bullying in schools. Even among unpopular and socially marginalized bullies, bullying may be viewed as a way of gaining status among one's peers. For example, unpopular, marginalized bullies are motivated to target victims in an effort to "gain the status that generally eludes them" (Rodkin, 2011, p. 12). While it is important to recognize that some bullies are unpopular and socially marginalized and have a "host of problems of which bullying behavior is but one manifestation" (Rodkin, 2011, p. 12), school personnel should not focus all their efforts on peripheral, antisocial cliques but should also focus their efforts on more socially connected and popular youth who may be responsible for a substantial number of bullying incidents in a school.

Are Witnesses Innocent Bystanders or Critical Players?

We are also beginning to acknowledge the critical role of peers who witness bullying incidents (Juvonen & Graham, 2004). The potential power of the bully is largely dependent on the reaction and behavior of peer witnesses (Rodkin, 2011). Rather than being "innocent bystanders," peer witnesses, who are present in the overwhelming majority (i.e., 85%–88%) of bullying incidents, play a critical role in diminishing, encouraging, or even prolonging bullying incidents (Swearer, Espelage, Vaillancourt, & Hymel, 2010; Vaillancourt, Hymel, & McDougall, 2003). Salmivalli, Kärnä, & Poskiparta's (2010) review of the literature on the group processes and group involvement in bullying reported that peer witnesses were often effective in ending a bullying episode when they intervened on behalf of the victim. For example, one study reported that 20% of witnesses defend the victim and attempt to stop the bullying and that these "defenders" are successful over 50% of the time (Salmivalli et al., 2010). Bystanders' reactions impact the victim's adjustment following a bullying episode. For example, one study found that victims who had one or more classmates defending them when victimized were less anxious, less depressed, and had a higher self-esteem than victims without defenders (Salmivalli et al., 2010). Despite the fact that many peer witnesses and bystanders believe that bullying is wrong and that defending their bullied peer would be the right thing to do, peer witnesses and bystanders rarely offer support to bullying victims (Salmivalli et al., 2010). Some of this reluctance to get involved may be explained by their desire to avoid being bullied themselves, despite the fact that youth who witness bullying often report increased feelings of guilt or helplessness for not confronting the bully and/or not supporting the victim (Hamburger et al., 2011). On the other hand, some peer witnesses actively convey support for the bully or even join in on the bullying (Pepler, 2001; Smith, Ananiadou & Cowie, 2003). Some peers have even reported being "excited," "energized," and "hyped" by the experience of witnessing peer-on-peer bullying (Kerbs & Jolley, 2007). Salmivalli et al. (2010) describes the dilemma facing witnesses and bystanders:

> The literature suggests that children and adolescents facing bullying problems as bystanders are trapped in a social dilemma. On one hand, they understand that bullying is wrong and they

would like to do something to stop it—on the other hand, they strive to secure their own status and safety in the peer group. However, *if fewer children rewarded and reinforced the bully, and if the group refused to assign high status for those who bully, an important reward for bullying others would be lost.* (p. 117)

The potential impact of peer witnesses and bystanders in combating bullying in schools is unmistakable. Based on these recent findings pointing to the importance of peer group dynamics on bullying, peer witnesses and bystanders appear to be an untapped resource in combating bullying in schools.

How Do Adults in School Perceive and Respond to Bullying?

It is important to recognize that teachers and administrators often seriously underestimate the extent to which bullying is a problem in their school as well as the role that they can play to prevent it (Kallestad & Olweus, 2003). This can be explained by several factors. First, the vast majority of bullying incidents in schools occur outside the view of adults (Vaillancourt, Hymel, & McDougall, 2003). For example, it has been estimated that teachers and administrators typically see only about 4% of bullying incidents (Kazdin & Rotella, 2009). Even when teachers witness bullying behavior, they often fail to recognize it as bullying behavior (Craig, Pepler, & Atlas, 2000; Cohn & Canter, 2003. For example, teachers and other adults may often overlook or dismiss the bullying behaviors of popular, high-status bullies because these students are liked by teachers and other adults (Vaillancourt, Hymel, & McDougall, 2003). Even when teachers or administrators witness bullying incidents, they don't always intervene, or they may even exacerbate the problem by blaming the victim (Rodkin & Hodges, 2003). Franks (2010) describes the various reasons why adults may not take action when they witness bullying in schools and the devastating implications of adult inaction or inconsistent action on victims:

> Teachers don't always take action because they receive little or no backup…or are fearful for their own physical safety. Principals are also often afraid of the parents of bullies, who are usually bullies themselves and who come tearing in, threatening lawsuits. In light of the new anti-bullying laws, principals fear the unwanted publicity will lead to a reduction of their school funding. And sometimes they are simply lazy. It is easier to ignore an incident, pretend it's just a part of growing up. As a result of this

lassitude—in school boards as well as individual schools—many adolescents come to believe that they deserve bullying. (p. 2)

Based on these facts, it should not be surprising that as few as 25%–30% of students who have been bullied report the incident to an authority figure (Smith & Shu, 2000; Unnever & Cornell, 2004). Moreover, adults' failure to take consistent action in response to bullying incidents may also impact students who witness bullying. In other words, if bullying behavior is wrong, why aren't adults stopping it?

Summary

I discuss bullying in all of its forms as a "systematic abuse of power" throughout this volume. Bullying is a specific type of aggression that involves an imbalance of power where the bully consciously intends to harm his or her victim physically and/or psychologically and has the power and the means to do so. It is important to be able to distinguish between bullying and other types of peer conflict, such as teasing. Teasing is not bullying because it is not intended to harm the other person. How the other person reacts to a teasing episode will largely determine how the interaction proceeds.

Recent research findings have increased our understanding of specific factors that contribute to bullying across a number of contexts, including individual characteristics, family characteristics, and a number of school characteristics. Bullying appears to be widespread in our public schools today with 39% of middle schools and 20% of elementary schools and high schools reporting that bullying occurs on a daily or weekly basis. However, it is also important to note that bullying statistics may seriously underestimate the true extent of bullying in schools. The most reliable predictor of becoming a bullying victim is being viewed as "not fitting in" or "being different" in some way. Bullying is no longer viewed as a normative phase that most children outgrow; rather, bullying is now linked to a broad range of long-term harmful effects including depression, loneliness, social anxiety, school phobia, and low self-esteem. Recent neuroscience research findings provide additional evidence that the short- and long-term impact of psychological forms of bullying can be as devastating for the victim as physical abuse. Youth who are bullied have also been show to be at greater risk of attempting suicide.

Rather than viewing bullies as misfits with low self-esteem, we are beginning to acknowledge that many school bullies have high self-esteem and a wide variety of friends, and are popular among their peers as a result of their social competence, physical attractiveness, and athleticism. Bullying is increasingly being viewed as a strategy for gaining or maintaining status among one's peers. We are also beginning to acknowledge the critical role of peers who witness bullying incidents, with the potential power of the bully largely dependent on the reaction and behavior of peer witnesses.

Teachers and administrators often seriously underestimate the extent to which bullying is a problem in their school as well as the role that they can play to prevent it. Even when teachers witness bullying behavior, they often fail to recognize it as bullying behavior, and they may even exacerbate the problem by blaming the victim. As a result, very few students who have been bullied report the incident to an authority figure.

3

■ ■ ■

Cyberbullying: Taking Bullying to New Levels of Cruelty

> Like an unchecked cancer, hate corrodes the personality and eats
> away its vital unity. Hate destroys a man's sense of values and his
> objectivity. It causes him to describe the beautiful as ugly and the
> ugly as beautiful, and to confuse the true with the false and the
> false with the true.
>
> —*Martin Luther King, Jr.*

This chapter begins with a discussion of the pervasive role of electronic
devices in the lives of today's youth. It defines cyberbullying and what we
currently know about the extent to which it occurs, the unique nature of
cyberbullying, and its impact among today's youth. It explores the unique
legal issues involved in combating cyberbullying. It discusses a number of
strategies designed to combat and prevent cyberbullying, including school-
based strategies, as well as interventions for families and communities. It
concludes with a discussion of strategies for making the Internet a place of
compassion and connection.

The Pervasive Role of Electronic Devices in the Lives of Today's Youth
Recent technological advances (e.g., increased affordability, mobile
interfaces) over the past decade have fundamentally altered the ways in
which teens communicate and interact with each other (Rivers, Chesney, &
Coyne, 2011). Today, between 93% and 97% of adolescents use the Internet,
and 80% have a mobile device that allows them to text-message and take
digital photos (Underwood & Rosen, 2011). Half of U.S. teens, between the
ages of 12 and 17, send 50 or more text messages a day, and one third send

more than 100 per day (Pew Research Center, 2010). American children and teens spend an average of 7 hours a day engaged with television, cell phones, handheld games, iPads, Internet games, Facebook, and video games (Benson, 2011). What is the impact of all this texting, instant messaging, and online social networking among today's youth? In addition to providing more opportunities for establishing and maintaining positive relationships with their peers, there are also more opportunities than ever for youth to harass and inflict harm on each other using a number of electronic devices.

What Is Cyberbullying?

Cyberbullying is the repeated use of computers, cell phones, and other electronic devices to harm, harass, humiliate, threaten, or damage the reputation and relationships of the intended victim. It involves "private (such as chat or text messaging), semi-public (such as posting a harassing message on an email list), or public communications (such as creating a website devoted to making fun of the victim)" (Schrock & Boyd, 2011, p. 374). It also includes "sexting," which is the act of sending sexually explicit messages or photographs, primarily between mobile phones (Center for Mental Health in Schools at UCLA, 2011; Hinduja & Patchin, 2007; Holladay, 2010). While a number of other terms (e.g., electronic bullying, e-bullying, online harassment, Internet bullying, and online social cruelty) are used in the literature to describe bullying through electronic devices (Hinduja & Patchin, 2009), for the purposes of this chapter, I will use the term "cyberbullying" to describe bullying through the use of electronic devices.

How Prevalent Is Cyberbullying Among Today's Children and Youth?

Unlike research on more traditional forms of face-to-face-bullying, research on cyberbullying is in its infancy. However, results from studies over the past several years are beginning to increase our understanding of the prevalence of cyberbullying among school-aged youth and young adults.

There is wide variation on the reported prevalence of cyberbullying among today's youth across research studies. Some of this variation is accounted for by the age range of the youth responding to the survey. Those studies that have explored reports of cyberbullying among middle and high school youth (ages 12–18) have found that 4% to 25% of youth have been cyberbullies or victims of cyberbullying. For example, the most recent national survey data on school violence and student safety from the National Center for Education Statistics (NCES) reported that 4% percent of youth, ages 12–18, had been cyberbullied in the year prior to the study (Robers, Zhang, & Truman, 2010), and the same NCES study indicates that about the same percentage of students had also been involved in the cyberbullying of other youth (Hinduja & Patchin, 2007) while another study reported that up to a quarter of middle and high school students are victims of cyberbullying (Cass & Anderson, 2011). Other studies have reported that 19% of middle schools and 18% of high schools experience daily or weekly problems with cyberbullying, either at school or away from school (Neiman, 2011). There is evidence that cyberbullying peaks around 13–14 years of age and that girls are more likely to be victims of cyberbullying than boys (Kowalski & Limber, 2007; Wang, Iannotti, & Nansel, 2009).

If the age range is expanded to include young adults (i.e., ages 18–24), the reported percentages of cyberbullying increase quite dramatically. For example, a recent study by Associated Press/MTV found that more than half (56%) of young people between the ages of 14 and 24 have been victims of cyberbullying, up from 50% in a similar 2009 MTV/AP survey (Kaufman, 2011). The percentage of young people who frequently see people being mean to each other on social networking sites also rose to 55% in the 2011 survey, up from 45% in a similar 2009 survey (Cass & Anderson, 2011).

Based on these findings, it appears that cyberbullying is a significant problem in our schools and communities. Given the fact that students' use of electronic communications technologies is "unlikely to wane in coming years" (Kowalski & Limber, 2007, p. S29), cyberbullying warrants the attention of school officials, parents, and community leaders. In fact, the CDC (Centers for Disease Control and Prevention) has identified all forms of electronic aggression as an emerging adolescent public health issue (David-Ferdon & Hertz, 2009).

What Is Important to Know About the Unique Nature of Cyberbullying?

Cyberbullies differ from face-to-face bullies in that cyberbullies can remain "virtually" anonymous by impersonating others or by hijacking another's account. Cyberbullies are not known by their victims almost half the time and cyberbullying often occurs off school grounds (Greene, 2006). The sharing or stealing of youths' private passwords occurs with relative frequency. For example, a 2001 Pew Internet research study found that 22% of teens between the ages of 12 and 17 had shared a password with a friend or with someone they knew (Schrock & Boyd, 2011). Another study found that 13%

of 4th–6th graders and 15% of 7th–9th graders experienced someone using their password without their permission (McQuade and Sampat, 2008). The ability to hide behind fake screen names or to steal someone else's screen name allows perpetrators to say things to each other that they would never say face-to-face "[and] may lead some perpetrators to remain unconvinced that they are actually harming their target [or that] they are doing anything wrong" (Kowalski & Limber, 2007, p. S28). As one kid stated "on Facebook, you can be as mean as you want" (Hoffman, 2010). Unlike face-to-face bullying that is limited to the immediate victim or bystanders, cyberbullies can spread their abuse across their entire electronic contact list in a matter of seconds, which may also serve to heighten victims' perceptions of vulnerability (Kowalski & Limber, 2007; Ollove, 2010). Perhaps most disturbing is that these harmful comments can be delivered at any time of the day or night by youth who cannot see the pain they are inflicting on their victims (Hinduja & Patchin, 2007; Underwood, Rish-Scott, & Springer, 2011).

One of the most challenging and distinct features of cyberbullying, compared with face-to-face bullying, is the degree to which parents and adults may not understand the nature or impact of cyberbullying. For example, many parents hold inaccurate beliefs about the risks their children face when they communicate online, parents underestimate the amount of information their children post online, and parents are often unaware of how online sites are used (DeHue, Bolman, & Völlink, 2008; Holladay, 2010; Rosen, Cheever, & Carrier, 2008). Many parents do not routinely supervise or monitor their teenager's electronic communications and also underestimate, to a significant degree, their child's involvement in making fun of a peer online (Holladay, 2010). Many parents also lag behind their children and teens in their understanding of and use of technology, which make cyberbullying incidents "very difficult for adults to detect or track" (Center for Mental Health in Schools at UCLA, 2011, p. 1).

An entirely new set of hostile behaviors is unique to cyberenvironments. These behaviors are identified and described in Table 3.1. Among these four bullying behaviors unique to cyberenvironments, it appears that *outing and trickery* and *picture or video clip bullying* are most common. For example, 20% of survey respondents reported someone sharing private information without their permission, and another 16% of respondents reported someone posting embarrassing pictures or videos of them without their permission (Cass & Anderson, 2011). However, it is important to note that sexting (or *picture or*

Table 3.1 Bullying Behaviors That Are Unique to Cyberenvironments

Term	Definition
Outing and trickery	Refers to convincing a target to reveal personal information and then sharing this private information with others electronically
Masquerading/impersonation	Refers to instances where a bully pretends to be the victim and then sends messages to others that seem to come from the victim. It also involves changing information the victim has posted about him/herself online
Happy slapping	Refers to digitally recording an episode of physical bullying/aggression and then electronically sharing this episode with others
Picture or video clip bullying	Entails the alteration of pictures and/or video clips of victims and then posting them for others to see in an effort to embarrass the victim

Note. *Source:* Adapted from Underwood & Rosen, 2011.

video clip bullying) appears to be much less common among minor children than previously thought. A recent study found that 10% of children between the ages of 10 and 17 have used a cell phone to send or receive sexually suggestive images and that only 1 in 100 has sent "images considered graphic enough to violate child pornography laws" (i.e., images that included full or partial nudity) (O'Connor, 2011).

Other forms of cyberbullying include the spreading of false rumors and the posting of "mean" messages on Internet pages or by text message (Cass & Anderson, 2011). Girls commonly target each other with labels such as "slut," "whore," and "bitch" while boys attack other boys a great deal for being "gay" or questioning their sexual orientation (Holladay, 2010; Wolak, Finkelhor, Mitchell, & Ybarra, 2008).

Several additional findings illustrate the uniqueness of cyberbullying compared with other forms of bullying. For example, there is some evidence that certain youths may be more likely to engage in cyberbullying or to be victimized by cyberbullying compared with other forms of bullying. Specifically, one study found that 64% of youth who reported being harassed online did not report being bullied in person (Ybarra, Diener-West, & Leaf, 2007). This may be due to the fact that socially anxious teens may find the Internet and related technologies as a means to communicate without fear or anxiety as well as a way to exact revenge on perpetrators of face-to-face bullying. While having more friends is a protective factor for face-to-face bullying, having more friends is not a protective factor against cyberbullying (Wang, Iannotti, & Nansel, 2009). Teens may also be more reluctant to report instances of electronic bullying since a report of electronic bullying may result in a restriction in cell phone or Internet use (Kowalski & Limber, 2007).

What Is the Impact of Cyberbullying?

Perhaps the most troubling aspect of cyberbullying is its potentially devastating impact on its victims. Cyberbullying is different from other forms of bullying due to its relentless nature. Victims cannot escape being cyberbullied. It can occur anywhere at any time. Cyberbullying takes bullying to new levels of cruelty and brutality because of a unique combination of factors. The combination of the typical adolescent's lack of impulse control and underdeveloped empathy skills combined with an online environment with no reference points to contain or regulate behavior can result in extreme forms of cruelty without any accompanying sense of guilt (Rivers, Chesney, & Coyne, 2011).

It has been reported that victims of cyberbullying experience a sense of worthlessness and disempowerment (Rivers, Chesney, & Coyne, 2011) and were more likely to use alcohol and drugs, earn lower grades, cheat at school, have absenteeism problems, assault others, damage property, and carry a weapon (Beran & Li, 2007). The link between cyberbullying and attempted suicide is particularly troubling. For example, cyberbullying victims were 1.9 times more likely to have attempted suicide (Hinduja & Patchin, 2010) than were others. The link between cyberbullying and suicide has been dramatically illustrated by several recent high-profile suicides involving young adults who were cyberbullied as a result of their sexual orientation (Schwartz, 2010).

Cyberbullies themselves have also reported experiencing hyperactivity, conduct problems, low prosocial behavior, frequent smoking and drunkenness, headaches, and not feeling safe at school (Sourander, et al., 2010) and were 1.5 times more likely to have attempted suicide (Hinduja & Patchin, 2010). Similar to the bully-victims described in Chapter 2 of this volume, the most troubled youth were those who are both cyberbullies and cybervictims. It has been estimated that between 3% and 12% of youth are both victims and perpetrators of cyberbullying (Beran & Li, 2007).

Cyberbullying, like more traditional forms of bullying, impacts the learning climate of the school. For example, rather than being able to explore valuable online resources for their academic work, "youths are constantly surveilling the landscape of cyberspace or real space to guard against problematic interpersonal encounters" (Hinduja & Patchin, 2007, p. 95). Cyberbullying may also lead to serious acts of school violence. For example, it has been reported that one in four youths frequently targeted by rumors and one in five youths frequently targeted by threats online carried a weapon to school at least once in the previous 30 days (Ybarra, Diener-West, & Leaf, 2007).

Legal Issues Involved in Combating Cyberbullying

The challenges that cyberbullying poses to school officials have resulted in increasing numbers of states amending state legislation to address cyberbullying among students. Thirty-six state laws now include language that prohibits cyberbullying, and 54% of states with bullying laws now include language that prohibits and specifically defines cyberbullying or electronic acts (Institute of Education Sciences, 2011).

Citing relevant court cases, Hinduja and Patchin (2011) argue that "educators have the authority to restrict expressions and discipline students for inappropriate speech or behavior that occurs at school if that speech causes a substantial disruption at school (Tinker), interference with the rights of students (Tinker), or is contrary to the school's educational mission (Fraser and Morse). Further, if that speech has created a hostile environment for a student, school personnel have the responsibility to [restrict that speech] (Davis)" (pp. 73–74).

However, cyberbullying presents particularly difficult legal challenges to school officials since infractions involving electronic communication almost always occur outside of school and particularly on weekends. Since students often engage in cyberbullying outside of the school setting using their own technology (Institute of Education Sciences, 2011), schools that impose disciplinary consequences for off-campus conduct have often faced legal challenges for violating students' rights to free speech (Hinduja & Patchin, 2011). In essence, the challenge facing educators in combating cyberbullying is finding a balance between freedom of speech and "the darker side of digital communication" (Holladay, 2010, p. 44).

An up-to-date review of state cyberbullying laws can be found at www.cyberbullying.us.

Strategies for Combating and Preventing Cyberbullying

While Chapter 6 of this volume describes a number of proven strategies for combating all forms of bullying in schools, efforts to combat cyberbullying must take into account its distinct characteristics. While many states and school districts are responding to cyberbullying with punitive responses that include suspensions, expulsions, and even criminal penalties, punitive discipline is often ineffective in combating cyberbullying (Janssen, 2010).

School-Based Strategies

As stated earlier, one of the most troubling aspects of cyberbullying is its impersonal nature. Specifically, the cyberbully cannot directly see the harm that he or she is inflicting on his or her victim, and when a perpetrator cannot see the facial expressions and reactions of his or her victim, increasing levels of viciousness and brutality often ensue. As a result, empathy training appears to be an important component of any effort to combat cyberbullying. A renewed focus on empathy is gaining the increasing attention of neuroscientists, psychologists, and educators who believe that developing empathy at an early age will lead to reductions in bullying and other kinds of violence. Empathy training involves two important components: (a) teaching children to understand their own feelings and behavior, and (b) having adults (parents and teachers) model empathetic behavior themselves. When children and youth are able to identify and label their own feelings and experience empathy themselves, they are more able to recognize and empathize with the feelings of others (Brody, 2010). Because empathy training includes a better understanding of emotional nuances and "reading" facial expressions and body language, it may deter students from engaging in cyberbullying (Ollove, 2010; Stout, 2010).

There is empirical evidence to support the inclusion of empathy training in cyberbullying interventions. A recent study by Ang & Goh (2010) explored the relationship between affective empathy, cognitive empathy, and gender on cyberbullying among a sample of 396 adolescents in Singapore. Based on their findings, the authors of this study concluded that "empathy training and education should be included in cyberbullying intervention programs, with additional emphasis on cognitive components of empathy for boys and affective components of empathy for girls" (p. 395).

A school-based program that emphasizes empathy training in combating cyberbullying is the *Middle School Cyberbullying Curriculum*. This curriculum, developed and implemented by the Seattle Public School District, educates teachers about cyberbullying and includes a language they can share with their students. It addresses the issue of a student being a bystander, a victim, or a bully at different times and how to resist the urge to "bully back." The curriculum focuses on writing and asks students to write personal contracts about their online behavior. It also involves parents by utilizing take-home letters and activities. It uses the following four promising prevention practices:

• Debunking misperceptions about digital behavior
• Building empathy and understanding
• Teaching online safety skills
• Equipping young people with strategies to reject digital abuse in their lives

Detailed information about the Middle School Cyberbullying Curriculum can be found at http://district.seattleschools.org/modules/cms/pages.phtml?pageid=216981.

A promising school-based prevention program that also focuses on empathy training is *Roots of Empathy*, a Canadian-based program. It is currently being implemented in about 3,000 elementary and middle schools in Canada and 40 schools in Seattle (Szalavitz, 2010). According to information from its website, *Roots of Empathy* is designed to "build caring, peaceful, and civil societies through the development of empathy in children and adults…at the heart of the program are classroom visits by an infant and parent…through guided observations of this loving relationship, children learn to identify and reflect on their own thoughts and feelings and those of others." Nine separate studies have shown that *Roots of Empathy* has helped reduce bullying at school and increased supportive behavior among students (Szalavitz, 2010). For more information see http://www.rootsofempathy.org/.

Strategies for Families

As stated earlier, many parents (a) do not routinely supervise or monitor their teenager's electronic communications, (b) are unaware of how online sites are used, and (c) also underestimate, to a significant degree, their child's involvement in making fun of a peer online. As a result, parents need to be much more proactive in monitoring the use of computers by their teenage children in the home. Delmonico & Griffin (2008) have outlined a number of strategies to assist parents in monitoring the use of computers by their teenage children in their home. These strategies include:

- Ensuring that the computer is only used in high-traffic areas within the home (e.g., family rooms, living rooms, kitchens) and not isolated in a teen's room, the basement, or the attic
- Limiting the days and times of use (e.g., not to be used after 11:00 p.m.; not available on Sundays)
- Using the computer only when responsible adults or siblings are nearby
- Ensuring that the monitor and open windows are visible to others when using the computer (e.g., facing monitor toward traffic areas, not minimizing windows as a parent passes by) (p. 439)

Delmonico and Griffin go on to state that it is "wise to involve e-teens in the development of these ideas since they are familiar with their online rituals that may lead to problematic behavior and be more invested in the implementation of these new strategies if they have been involved in their development" (p. 439). It is also important for parents to be aware of Web sites where cyberbullying is promoted and occurs with great frequency (e.g., Formspring, TOPIX, 4 CHAN, My Yearbook).

Parents can also use the vehicle of reality television to teach tolerance and empathy to their teenage children. *If You Really Knew Me* is an American reality television series on MTV that focuses on youth subculture and different cliques in high schools. In each episode, students from each clique participate in Challenge Day, where students from all walks of life gather together in one room where each student must reveal something personal about him or herself. It's at this point where each student begins his/her dialogue with the words "If you really knew me . . . " The goal of Challenge Day is to demonstrate to students the possibility of love and connection through the celebration of diversity, truth, and full expression. The show focuses on Challenge Day in various high schools. Discussion guides for each episode can be found at http://www.challengeday.org/mtv/.

Community Interventions

Since cyberbullying extends beyond the school, interventions should also extend beyond the school to include the surrounding community. Community-level interventions refer to change efforts that strive to shift the underlying infrastructure within a community or targeted context to support a desired outcome, including shifting existing policies and practices, resource allocations, relational structures, community norms and values, and skills and attitudes (Durlak et al., 2007). One of the most promising approaches for involving communities in addressing problems impacting teens, such as bullying, is Communities That Care (CTC). The CTC, developed by Drs. J. David Hawkins and Richard Catalano at the University of Washington's Social Development Research Group (SDRG), uses a public health approach and rigorous research findings from prevention science to engage community stakeholders and decision makers in understanding and applying information about risk and protective factors that can buffer young people from problematic behaviors and promote positive youth development (Fagan, Hawkins, & Catalano, 2008; Hawkins, Catalano, & Associates, 1992). More detailed information about CTC can be found at http://ncadi.samhsa.gov/features/ctc/resources.aspx.

Making the Internet a Place of Compassion and Connection

An innovative strategy to specifically combat cyberbullying is making the Internet a place of social connection and compassion rather than a place of aggression. Blog sites such as 37 Days (an exploration of what would matter to us if we only had 37 days to live), Lifeline Gallery (stories of hope and recovery to raise awareness about the effects of suicide and connect people to social support), and AllDayBuffet (a site that promotes social action) are examples of sites focusing on connection and compassion (Martin, 2008). The social media (e.g., Facebook and Twitter) also provide outlets for connecting teens in productive and positive ways. These include the Charter for Compassion (see http://www.facebook.com/CharterforCompassion) and the Compassionate Friends/USA and CompSocieties.

Summary

Cyberbullying is the repeated use of computers, cell phones, and other electronic devices to harm, harass, humiliate, threaten, or damage the reputation and relationships of the intended victim. Between 4% and 25% of youth have been cyberbullies or victims of cyberbullying, and more than half (56%) of young people between the ages of 14 and 24 have been victims of cyberbullying. The Centers for Disease Control and Prevention have identified all forms of electronic aggression as an emerging adolescent public health issue.

Cyberbullies differ from face-to-face bullies in several ways: they can remain "virtually" anonymous by impersonating others or hijacking another's account, they can spread their abuse across their entire electronic contact list in a matter of seconds, and they cannot see the pain they are inflicting on their victims. Many parents and adults do not understand the nature or impact of cyberbullying and do not routinely supervise or monitor's their teenager's electronic communications. Cyberbullying is also distinct from other forms of bullying due to its relentless nature.

An entirely new set of hostile behaviors is unique to cyberenvironments. There is some evidence that certain youths may be more likely to engage in cyberbullying or to be victimized by cyberbullying compared with other forms of bullying. While having more friends is a protective factor for face-to-face bullying, having more friends is not a protective factor against cyberbullying. Teens may also be more reluctant to report instances of electronic bullying since a report of electronic bullying may result in a restriction in cell phone or Internet use.

Cyberbullying has a potentially devastating impact on its victims. It has been reported that victims of cyberbullying experience a sense of worthlessness and disempowerment. The link between cyberbullying and attempted suicide is particularly troubling. Cyberbullying may also lead to serious acts of school violence. For example, it has been reported that one in four youths frequently targeted by rumors and one in five youths frequently targeted by threats online carried a weapon to school at least once in the previous 30 days.

Thirty-six state laws now include language that prohibits cyberbullying, and 54% of states with bullying laws now include language that prohibits and specifically defines cyberbullying or electronic acts. The primary challenge facing educators in combating cyberbullying is finding a balance between freedom of speech and "the darker side of digital communication."

Empathy training appears to be an important component of any effort to combat cyberbullying. The *Middle School Cyberbullying Curriculum* and *Roots of Empathy* are two programs that include empathy-training components. It is also important for parents to utilize several strategies to monitor the use of computers by their teenage children in their home. One of the most promising approaches for involving communities in addressing problems impacting teens, such as bullying, is Communities That Care. It is also important to make the Internet a place of social connection and compassion rather than a place of aggression.

4

■ ■ ■

LGBTQ Bullying and Sexual Bullying in Schools

We must never assume that justice is on the side of the strong.
The use of power must always be accompanied by moral choice.
—*Theodore Bikel*

This chapter discusses the prevalence of LGBT bullying, how school personnel respond to LBGT bullying, the impact of bullying based on known or presumed gay or lesbian sexual orientation, and school-based strategies that minimize or prevent antigay bullying. It identifies and discusses several religious and political dimensions of LGBT bullying and offers strategies for acknowledging and addressing these religious and political issues. The chapter then turns to the nature and extent of sexual bullying/harassment in schools and the impact of sexual bullying/harassment on victims and discusses programs and strategies for preventing sexual bullying/harassment in schools.

This chapter will refer to both the LGBT population and the LGBTQ population in various places. This is because some studies have focused exclusively on the LGBT population while others focus more broadly on the LGBTQ population. LGBT refers to lesbian, gay, bisexual, and transgender youth, and the "Q" refers to youth questioning their sexuality or youth who experience same-sex physical and romantic attraction but who do not self-identify (Moe, Leggett, & Perera-Diltz, 2011). Sexual orientation is defined as the direction of emotional, cognitive, and sexual attraction and its expression, including heterosexuality, homosexuality, bisexuality, and asexuality.

Gender expression is defined as all the external characteristics and behaviors socially defined as either masculine or feminine, including dress, mannerisms, speech patterns, and social interactions. Homophobia is defined as a dislike, mistrust, or hatred of gays and lesbians. Transphobia is defined as a dislike, mistrust, or hatred of transgendered persons. Heterosexism is defined as the assumption that heterosexuality is the only valid, or even existing, form of sexual identity or family life.

Prevalence of LGBT Bullying

LGBT students face unrelenting bullying and harassment by their peers in many U.S. schools (U.S. Department of Health and Human Services, n.d.,b). A 2009 national survey conducted by Gay, Lesbian, and Straight Education Network (GLSEN) (2010) that involved over 7,000 LGBT students between the ages of 13 and 21 provides ample evidence of the onslaught of verbal and physical bullying. The authors of this GLSEN study found that 84.6% of LGBT were verbally harassed (e.g., called names or threatened) at school because of their sexual orientation, and 63.7% were verbally harassed because of their gender expression; 40.1% of LGBT students were physically harassed (e.g., pushed or shoved) at school in the past year because of their sexual orientation, and 27.2% were physically harassed because of their gender expression; 18.8% of LGBT students were physically assaulted (e.g., punched, kicked, injured with a weapon) because of their sexual orientation, and 12.5% were physically assaulted because of their gender expression; 52.9% of LGBT students were harassed or threatened by their peers via electronic mediums (e.g., text messages, e-mail, instant messages or postings on Internet sites such as Facebook); 88.9% of LGBT students heard "gay" used in a negative way (e.g., "that's so gay") frequently or often at school; 72.4% of LGBT students heard other homophobic remarks (e.g., "dyke" or "faggot") frequently or often at school; 62.6% of LGBT students heard negative remarks about gender expression frequently or often at school. Diaz, Kosciw, & Greytak (2010) found that transgender students experience higher rates of in-school victimization and lower levels of school connectedness than lesbian, gay, and bisexual students who are not transgender. The authors of the GLSEN (2010) study reported that LGBT students' experiences with more severe forms of bullying and harassment (i.e., physical assault and physical harassment) have remained relatively constant since 1999.

Sanders (2010) powerfully describes the psychic terror facing LGBT students everyday in our public schools. He states:

> ...every LGBT person is always and everywhere at risk of becoming the target of violence solely because of sexual orientation or gender identity...beyond the inflicting of individual pain, violence against lesbian, gay, bisexual, and transgender people has effects far beyond the individual target...while a majority of LGBT people may avoid ever becoming the victim of a violence, none will be able to avoid the psychic terror that is visited upon LGBT people with each reminder that this world is one in which people are maimed and killed because of their sexual and gender identities. It is this psychic terror that makes life so difficult for many LGBT people. It is this psychic terror that does the heavy lifting of instrumental, systematic violence. It intends to silence and to destroy from within. (para. 10)

It should also be noted that straight students who do not conform to socially defined characteristics and behaviors (i.e., not acting "masculine enough" or "feminine enough") also face relentless bullying in our schools. For example, it has been estimated that for every lesbian, gay, and bisexual youth who is bullied, four straight students who are perceived to be gay or lesbian are bullied (National Mental Health Association, 2002).

How Do School Personnel Respond to LGBTQ Bullying?

Eighty percent of a national sample of gay students reported that school employees do little or nothing to stop antigay behavior when they witness it (Gould, 2011), and 34% of LGBT victims who did report a bullying incident stated that school staff did nothing in response to their report (GLSEN, 2010). Not surprisingly, over half (62%) of the victims of bullying based on sexual orientation or gender expression did not report the incident to adults in school because they believed that little or no action would be taken or that the situation could become worse if reported (GLSEN, 2010).

Impact of Bullying Based on Known or Presumed Gay or Lesbian Sexual Orientation

This relentless verbal and sometimes physical bullying has a significant impact on the mental health and school performance of LGBT victims. Compared with heterosexual and gender-conforming youth, LGBTQ youth experience higher levels of isolation, runaway behavior, homelessness, domestic violence, anxiety, violent victimization, substance abuse, and pregnancy (National Association of Pediatric Nurse Practitioners [NAPNAP], 2011). LGBTQ youth are also more than twice as likely as their heterosexual peers to be depressed, engage in self-harming behavior, and think about or attempt suicide (Russell & Joyner, 2002). In fact, suicide remains the third leading cause of death of LGBT youth (D'Augelli et al., 2005).

Being victimized in school because of one's sexual orientation or gender expression also impacts school performance in several important ways. Table 4.1 summarizes the latest research findings on the impact of LGBT bullying on school performance. As seen in Table 4.1, LGBT students who are victims of chronic bullying do not feel safe at school and, therefore, miss a lot of school, which often leads to lower academic grades and lower GPAs. There is also

Table 4.1 Impact of GLBT Bullying on School Performance

	Compared With Other Students, Many Victims of GLBT Bullying
Do not feel safe at school	Three times as many victims of GLBT bullying reported feeling unsafe at school compared with non-LGBT students (20% vs. 6%). Sixty-one percent of LGBT students felt unsafe at school because of their sexual orientation, and 39.9% felt unsafe because of how they expressed their gender.
Miss a lot of school	Three times as many victims of GLBT bullying missed classes (29.1% vs. 8.0%), and they were four times likelier to have missed at least one day of school (30.0% vs. 6.7%) in the past month compared with the general population of secondary school students.
Have lower levels of educational achievement and lower educational aspirations	LGBT students who were frequently harassed because of their sexual orientation or gender expression had grade point averages almost half a grade lower than students who were less often harassed (2.7 vs. 3.1). LGBT students were also more likely to report that they did not plan to pursue any type of postsecondary education or obtain a high school diploma compared with a national sample of students (9.9% vs. 6.6%).

Note. *Sources:* GLSEN, 2010; Harris Interactive and GLSEN, 2005.

evidence that bullying negatively impacts LGBT students' long-term educational aspirations.

School-Based Strategies That Minimize or Prevent Antigay Bullying

There is growing evidence that several concrete steps can be taken by school officials to minimize antigay bullying in schools and create a more welcoming and safe environment for LGBTQ students (see Box 4.1).

First and foremost, every school should establish a gay–straight alliance (GSA). GSAs provide a safe haven and critical support for LGBT students, particularly in schools where there is a hostile climate toward LGBT students (Diaz et al., 2010; Kosciw, Diaz, & Greytak, 2008; Szalacha, 2003). Toomey, Ryan, Diaz, & Russell (2011) found that the presence of a high school GSA was associated with better young adult well-being as well as more college-level educational attainment and that their study "builds on prior work by documenting that the existence of a GSA has a positive influence on the lives of LGBT young people. Our findings have implications for school-based personnel in that they provide one avenue through which professionals may offer and support a positive school environment for LGBT young people. Schools should support these school-based clubs given that they offer the potential for positive development and greater educational

---

Box 4.1 School-Based Strategies That Have Been Shown to Minimize or Prevent Antigay Bullying in Schools

Gay–straight alliances—Student-run clubs in high schools or middle schools that bring together LGBTQ and straight students to support each other, provide a safe place to socialize, and create a platform for activism to fight homophobia and transphobia.

Supportive educators—LGBTQ youth should have knowledge of and access to at least one supportive adult in the school.

Comprehensive bullying/harassment policies—Sexual orientation, gender identity, and gender expression should be explicitly included in schools' antibullying policies.

Inclusive curriculum—Positive representations of LGBT people and the achievements of gays and lesbians throughout history should be incorporated in school curricula.

---

attainment" (p. 184). The Gay-Straight Alliance Network is a youth leadership organization that connects school-based gay–straight alliances to each other and community resources through peer support, leadership development, and training. The GSA Network supports young people in starting, strengthening, and sustaining GSAs. Detailed information about the GSA Network can be found at http://www.gsanetwork.org/.

Having the support of and access to supportive educators is also important. Victims of anti-LGBTQ bullying who feel they have the support of and access to at least one adult are more likely to feel safer while at school, to miss less school, and to report bullying (Kosciw et al., 2008; Moe et al., 2011; Russell, Seif, & Truong, 2001). The presence of supportive educators can have a significant positive impact on LGBT students' psychological well-being and longer-term educational aspirations (GLSEN, 2010).

Since there is currently no federal law that prohibits discrimination based on sexual orientation at school (Shah, 2011), a third strategy involves the development and enforcement of comprehensive bullying/harassment policies. Comprehensive policies send a message that the safety of all students, including LGBTQ students, is taken seriously by school administrators and that bias-based bullying and harassment will not be tolerated in the school (Diaz et al., 2010). Schools that have already implemented comprehensive antibullying policies that explicitly include sexual orientation, gender identity, and gender expression have seen increased rates of staff intervention and lower rates of LGBTQ bullying (GLSEN, 2010; Shah, 2011). The current absence of a federal law prohibiting discrimination based on sexual orientation at school has led Senator Al Franken (D-MN) to propose the inclusion of the Student Non-Discrimination Act, which includes specific language to protect students from being bullied because of their sexual orientation, as part of the reauthorization of the Elementary and Secondary Education Act. Senator Franken's legislation is in addition to the Safe Schools Improvement Act, proposed by Sens. Casey (D-PA) and Kirk (R-IL), which would "require schools and districts that accept federal funds to establish codes of conduct that specifically prohibit bullying and harassment for any reason, including for students' sexual orientation and gender identity" (Shah, 2011, p. 14).

A fourth strategy is an inclusive school curriculum that incorporates the achievements of gays and lesbians throughout history as well as positive representations of LGBT people, history, and events. This type of inclusive curriculum has been shown to improve an individual LGBT student's school experiences and school connectedness (GLSEN, 2010; Hart & Parmeter, 1992; Linsley, 2001). Schools can also provide age-appropriate instruction on sexual orientation in health and sexuality curricula (GLSEN, n.d.). Schools should also ensure that the guidance department and school library include pamphlets and books that contain age-appropriate and accurate information about the LGBTQ population (Hart & Parmeter, 1992; Linsley, 2001). Accurate and truthful information about sexual orientations and gender expression "helps students to understand and respect people who may seem 'different', an essential lesson for ensuring stability in our diverse society" (Macgillivray, 2004, p. 149).

Religious and Political Dimensions of LGBTQ Bullying

Several religious and political issues must be acknowledged before attempting to move forward and implement any of the previously mentioned strategies to combat antigay bullying in schools and create a more welcoming and safe environment for LGBTQ students. This is especially true in communities where there is intolerance toward gays and lesbians.

Much antigay bullying in schools stems from the systemic problems of homophobia and heterosexism. In many schools and communities, heterosexuality is viewed as "...'normal' and 'natural' not only through gender socialization but through construction of sexual otherness as inferior" (Walton, 2004, p. 26). While many school administrators heartily embrace antibullying strategies, antibullying initiatives that avoid the larger systemic issues of homophobia and heterosexism enhance the safety of some students but leave some of the most vulnerable students "unsafe" where the "...threat of violence for gender and sexual orientation nonconformity is pervasive" (Walton, 2004, p. 29). The reach and devastating impact of homophobic bullying is pointedly described by Parsons (2005):

> With homophobic bullying, you are either one of 'us' or one of 'them'. Anyone defending a target labeled 'gay' is in danger of being labeled the same. In fact, gay and lesbian students will often resort to homophobic bullying to deflect suspicions about their own sexual orientation...[and] adults who are proactive in confronting homophobia are subject to whisper campaigns about their own sexual orientation. (p. 23)

Much opposition to LGBT equality also stems from moral conservatives and their deeply held fundamentalist religious beliefs. Central among these beliefs is that the Bible is the literal word of God and that there are moral absolutes and premarital sex and homosexuality are condemned (Putnam & Campbell, 2010). As a result, strong objections have been raised by religious conservatives and fundamentalists regarding any antibullying strategy that includes LGBT students as victims. Leaders from religious right organizations such as the Moral Majority, the Christian Coalition, and Focus on the Family have actively opposed any efforts to combat antigay bullying in schools because they view these efforts as a way of legitimizing and promoting homosexuality as "normal and natural" (Macgillivray, 2004, p. 17). Focus on the Family contends that liberals and gay rights groups are using the anti-LGBTQ bullying banner to pursue a hidden agenda designed to sneak homosexuality into classrooms to indoctrinate and recruit students (Cushman, 2010; People for the American Way, n.d.). Focus on the Family education expert Candi Cushman argues that activists are using their antibullying rhetoric to convey that homosexuality is normal and should be accepted while opposing viewpoints by conservative Christians are portrayed as bigotry and belittled (Macgillivray, 2004). Morally conservative parents believe that parental rights and religious freedoms are in danger of being violated when "homosexual activism" is promoted in schools (Cushman, 2010). However, Eliza Byard, executive director of the national Gay, Lesbian, and Straight Education Network, says its agenda is to "ensure safe schools and acceptance for all students, regardless of sexual orientation, gender identity, religion, race, national origin or ability" (Draper, 2010, para. 7). While conservative parents believe that there should be no tolerance of bullying, they believe that gay rights groups are using the gay rights issue to press a social agenda (Eckholm, 2011b).

Unfortunately, school personnel are often caught in the middle of this intense political and religious battle. Most teachers have expressed a strong commitment to safeguard LGBT students and to work to create school climates that are safe and supportive (Harris Interactive and GLSEN, 2005). However, teachers also do not want to violate the rights of morally conservative parents who do not want their children to view or treat homosexuality as a socially acceptable lifestyle (Macgillivray, 2004). School officials may also be hindered in their efforts to protect LGBT students out of fear of a substantial backlash from these conservative parents and religious right organizations. For example, school officials may resist allowing students to form gay–straight alliances, or they may subject GSAs to a different set of rules (Harris Interactive and GLSEN, 2005).

Not surprisingly, a central battleground in this fight between morally conservative parents and school officials is centered upon proposals to include sexual orientation in schools' nondiscrimination policies. Conservative parents and religious right organizations believe that the ultimate result will be the legitimization and promotion of homosexuality as an acceptable alternative to heterosexuality and will also result in LGBT students and staff having "special rights" (Macgillivray, 2004). However, it can also be argued that a school district's attempt to remain neutral on the bullying of LGBT students "is inherently stigmatizing" because it inhibits teachers and other adults from "confronting destructive stereotypes" and responding aggressively to the bullying of LGBT students and results in "a toxic environment" for LGBT students (Eckholm, 2011, p. 3). (A broader discussion of religious bullying, which extends beyond the targeting of LGBT students, can be found in Chapter 5 of this volume.)

Addressing Religious and Political Issues Surrounding LGBTQ Bullying

Most importantly, the objections of religious conservatives and funda-mentalists regarding the bullying of LGBTQ students should not be ignored or dismissed. It is important to be sensitive to and respectful of strongly held religious beliefs because, when this occurs, the groups holding these beliefs are more likely to be receptive to change (Cole, 2006). Instead, each of their arguments and concerns should be directly addressed and myths should be replaced by facts. One of the major objections of religious conservatives is that combating LGBT bullying in schools will result in students being recruited and brainwashed to "become gay." However, there is considerable scientific evidence that an individual's sexual orientation is not a choice (American Psychological Association, 2011). Opponents also argue that anti-LGBT bullying provides special rights to LGBT students. However, protecting LGBT students from bullying simply ensures that LGBT students receive similar protections against harassment as other groups of students (e.g., students with disabilities) (People for the American Way, n.d.). Focus on the Family contends that generic antibullying policies that don't include LGBT bullying are most effective, but they offer no evidence to substantiate this claim. However, there is evidence that schools become safer for *all* students when schools adopt antibullying policies that enumerate the categories of students most frequently targeted by bullies, including race, religion, disability, sexual orientation, and gender identity or expression (Costello, 2010b).

Since scientific evidence alone is not likely to influence or sway the opinions of individuals whose negative views about homosexuality are based on their religious beliefs, arguments should also be theological in nature (Bartkowski, 1996). Some religious leaders have offered compelling counterarguments to the biblical basis for antigay beliefs. (For example, see Daniel Helminiak's book *What the Bible Really Says About Homosexuality.*)

The bottom line is that groups of people with differing religious beliefs must learn to cope with each other in our democratic society as well as work together to protect all students from being harmed. Costello (2010b), writing on behalf of Teaching Tolerance, argues these points forcefully and effectively:

> Focus on the Family's biggest fear is that schools will reflect a diverse U.S. society—one that includes LGBT students. They do not want to be challenged in their belief that homosexuality is immoral, abnormal and changeable. We don't expect to change those personal beliefs. Simply put, our goal is to ask those who would ignore the pain and suffering of these children to understand that acknowledging the problem of anti-gay bullying—and wanting to make schools safe for all students from harassment—doesn't require that you approve . . . we would remind them that living in a democratic and diverse society means living alongside people with whom you disagree. The alternative is to stay silent and stand by while terrible things happen to other people's children. Terrible things that no parent would ever want to happen to his or her own child. (p. 2)

Sexual Bullying/Harassment

Sexual bullying and sexual harassment are used in the literature to describe verbal or physical conduct of a sexual nature. The concept of sexual harassment is distinct from the concept of sexual bullying in several ways. Most significantly, sexual harassment is a form of sex discrimination and is illegal under federal law Title IX, which was passed by the U.S. Congress in 1972 (Stein & Mennemeier, 2011). Sexual bullying, as codified in state laws, varies state by state and does not rise to the level of being a violation of federal law (Stein & Mennemeier, 2011).

While a number of researchers detail the important differences between sexual harassment and sexual bullying (see Sparks, 2011, and see Espelage,

Stein, Rose, & Elliot, 2009), I will use the terms *sexual bullying* and *sexual harassment* interchangeably throughout this chapter since I agree with the view that sexual harassment is "bullying with overt sexual overtones" (Stein & Mennemeier, 2011).

In the broadest sense, sexual bullying/harassment is any form of physical or nonphysical bullying using a person's sexuality or gender as a weapon by boys or girls toward other boys or girls—although it is more commonly directed at girls (NSPCC, n.d.). It includes bullying people because of their sex life (e.g., because they haven't had sex or because they've had sex with a number of people), or their body (e.g., the size of their breasts). It includes using words that refer to someone's sexuality in a derogatory way (like calling something "gay" to mean that it is not very good), using sexual words to put someone down (like calling someone "slut" or "bitch"), making threats or jokes about serious and frightening subjects like rape, spreading rumors about someone's sexuality and sex life, touching parts of someone's body where he or she doesn't want to be touched, and putting pressure on someone to act in a sexual way (NSPCC).

What Is the Nature and Extent of Sexual Bullying/Harassment in Schools?

A 2011 national study on sexual harassment in schools sponsored by the American Association of University Women (AAUW) provides up-to-date findings on the extent to which students in Grades 7–12 have experienced or witnessed sexual harassment in schools (Hill & Kearl, 2011). In this survey, sexual harassment was defined as unwelcome sexual behavior that takes place in person or electronically; if everyone involved likes and agrees to the sexual behavior, it is not sexual harassment. The authors of this study reported the following findings: Nearly half (48%) of the students surveyed experienced some form of sexual harassment with verbal harassment (unwelcome sexual comments, jokes, or gestures) making up the bulk of the incidents. Sexual harassment by text, e-mail, Facebook, or other electronic means affected 30% of students, and many of the students who were sexually harassed through cyberspace were also sexually harassed in person. Girls were more likely than boys to be sexually harassed (56% versus 40%). Girls and boys reported that they were called *gay* or *lesbian* in a negative way in equal numbers (18% of students). One third of girls (33%) and about one quarter (24%) of boys said that they observed sexual harassment at their school. Among students who were sexually harassed, about 9% reported the incident to a teacher, guidance counselor, or other adult at school, and about one quarter (27%) of students said they talked about the incident with parents or family members (including siblings); about one quarter (23%) spoke with friends about the incident; and one half of students who were sexually harassed said they did nothing afterward in response to sexual harassment. Forty-four percent who admitted to sexually harassing others didn't think of it as a big deal, and 39% said they were trying to be funny; only a handful of students who harassed others did so because they wanted a date with the person (3%) or thought the person liked it (6%). Ninety-two percent of girls and 80% of boys who admitted to sexually harassing another student were also the target of sexual harassment themselves (Hill & Kearl, 2011). Other researchers have reported that cyberbullying (discussed in detail in Chapter 3 of this volume) is emerging as the newest way to sexually harass peers, with 18% of students reporting that a harassing text message was sexual in nature (Ybarra, Espelage, & Martin, 2011), and that sexual harassment is more severe in high school than in middle school (Gruber & Fineran, 2008).

It is important to note that teachers and other adults may also bully and harass students in sexual ways. It is difficult to know the actual rate of teachers as abusers because the sexual abuse often goes unreported. However, an extensive investigation by the Associated Press found that 2,570 teaching credentials were revoked between 2001 and 2005 for allegations of sexual misconduct with a student (Irvine & Tanner, 2007). Most allegations of sexual abuse by teachers are often unfounded or declared false due to "insufficient evidence" and a victim's morality comes into question (Irvine & Tanner, 2007). (A detailed discussion of additional ways that teachers bully students can be found of Chapter 5 of this volume.)

Impact of Sexual Bullying/Harassment on Victims

While both girls and boys can encounter sexual harassment at school, it appears that sexual harassment is a highly gendered phenomenon that is directly associated with negative outcomes for girls (Hill & Kearl, 2011). While the vast majority of victims (87%) said it had a negative effect on them, girls are more likely than boys to say that sexual harassment caused them to have trouble sleeping (22% of girls vs. 14% of boys), not want to go to school (37% of girls vs. 25% of boys), or change the way they went to school or back home from school (10% of girls vs. 6% of boys). Girls were more likely in every case to say they felt that way for "quite a while" compared with boys. Boys were most likely to report that being called *gay* was the type of sexual harassment most troubling to them. Reactions varied, however, with some boys saying that they laughed it off, while others expressed embarrassment, sadness, or fear as a result of the experience (Hill & Kearl, 2011). It has also been reported that the effects of sexual harassment in high school are more damaging than the bullying behaviors students may have experienced in middle school (Gruber & Fineran, 2008).

Preventing Sexual Bullying/Harassment in Schools

Based on these findings, prevention efforts should focus on situations where humor crosses the line and becomes sexual harassment (Hill & Kearl, 2011). Students who participated in the 2011 AAUW study of sexual harassment in schools offered several ideas for reducing sexual harassment in their school, including: designating a person students can talk to; providing online resources; holding in-class discussions; and providing for the anonymous reporting of problems, enforcement of sexual harassment policies, and punishment of harassers. Based on findings from their national survey as well as other researchers in this field, Hill & Kearl (2011) also offer a number of concrete recommendations to combat sexual bullying and harassment in schools (see Box 4.2). In essence, by viewing sexual bullying as harassment, school districts can take specific actions based on the federal definition of sexual harassment and the rights of students under Title IX (Goodemann, Zammitt, & Hagedorn, in press).

Several programs show promise in reducing sexual bullying and harassment in schools. Expect Respect: A School-Based Program Promoting Safe and Healthy Relationships for Youth was developed in the late 1980s by SafePlace. According to information contained on their Web site, a major premise of the Expect Respect program is that bullying and sexual harassment behaviors condition students to accept mistreatment in their peer relationships, laying the foundation for abuse in future dating relationships. Without effective adult intervention, students learn to expect and accept mistreatment from and among their peers. Based upon available research on bullying, the most effective strategy involves preparing all members of the school community to respond consistently whenever a student is mistreated (Olweus, Limber, & Mihalic, 1999). The Expect Respect program consists of four components: (a) counseling and support groups, (b) classroom presentations, (c) the summer teen leadership program, and (d) training for school personnel. According to the publication, *Expect Respect: A School-Based Program Promoting Safe &*

Box 4.2 Recommendations Designed to Combat Sexual Bullying and Harassment in Schools

- Schools that do not have a sexual harassment policy must create one, and all schools should make sure that the policy is publicized and enforced.
- Schools must ensure that students are aware of and educated about what sexual harassment is, what their rights are under Title IX, and how to respond if they experience or witness sexual harassment.
- Schools must train their staff and faculty to recognize and respond to sexual harassment, to know how to help students who come to them, and to know their obligations if they witness sexual harassment.
- Schools must work to create a culture of respect and gender equality.
- Schools must teach all students that sexual harassment is not funny.
- Schools must create a culture of acceptance and tolerance for all, without regard to gender presentation or sexual orientation, and must reinforce that culture by the attitudes, words, and actions of school officials, faculty, and staff.
- Schools must recognize and address how the intersections of race, class, gender, and sexual orientation can cause some students to fare worse than others when they experience sexual harassment.
- Schools must teach students about cyberharassment, what their rights are, and how to respond to or report instances.

Source: Hill, C., & Kearl, H. (2011). *Crossing the line: Sexual harassment at school*. Washington, DC: American Association of University Women. Reprinted with permission.

Healthy Relationships for Youth by Barri Rosenbluth, published by the National Resource Center on Domestic Violence, intervention schools demonstrated a decrease in students' self-reported incidences of bullying others, being bullied, and witnessing bullying; and students' acceptance of negative dating and gender role attitudes as well as an increase in students' willingness to intervene on behalf of other students who were being bullied or harassed, students' ability to identify sexual harassment, students' awareness of school sexual harassment policy, and students' willingness to tell parents and adults on campus about incidents of bullying and sexual harassment.

Shifting Boundaries: Lessons on Relationships for Students in Middle School was developed by Nan D. Stein, with Kelly Mennemeier, Natalie Russ, and Bruce Taylor, with contributions from the New York City Department of Education. Shifting Boundaries began in 2005 and features detailed instructions for teachers and handouts for six sessions for Grades 6 and 7. The lessons discuss setting boundaries, measuring personal space, determining appropriate and inappropriate behaviors at school, what sexual harassment is, how to respond, the consequences for harassers, and mapping safe and unsafe spaces at school. Each lesson includes discussion questions, group work, and personal reflection. In one activity, students map out "hot spots" in the school where they feel most unsafe. A 2010 study funded by the U.S. Department of Justice of 30 New York City middle schools found schools that implemented the program saw 26% to 34% fewer instances of sexual harassment after 6 months, 32% to 47% fewer instances of sexual violence, and 50% less physical and sexual dating violence than at the start of the program.

Summary

LGBT students face unrelenting bullying and harassment by their peers in many U.S. schools. Gay students report that school employees do little or nothing to stop antigay behavior when they witness it. LGBT students who are victims of chronic bullying do not feel safe at school, miss a lot of school, and get lower academic grades and lower GPAs. Suicide remains the third leading cause of death of LGBT youth.

Several concrete steps can be taken by school officials to minimize antigay bullying in schools: establish a gay–straight alliance; ensure that LGBTQ youth have knowledge of and access to at least one supportive adult in the school; develop and enforce an antibullying policy that explicitly includes sexual orientation, gender identity, and gender expression; and incorporate positive representations of LGBT people and the achievements of gays and lesbians throughout history in the school curriculum.

Much opposition to LGBT equality stems from moral conservatives and their deeply held fundamentalist religious beliefs. Unfortunately, school personnel are often caught in the middle of this intense political and religious battle. For example, while most teachers want to protect LGBTQ students from being bullied, teachers also do not want to violate the rights of morally conservative parents.

Sexual bullying and sexual harassment is any form of physical or nonphysical bullying using a person's sexuality or gender as a weapon by boys or girls toward other boys or girls—although it is more commonly directed at girls. Nearly half of the students in a national survey experienced some form of sexual harassment, with verbal harassment making up the bulk of the incidents. Teachers and other adults bully and harass students in sexual ways but it often goes unreported. Intervention efforts should focus on situations where humor crosses the line and becomes sexual harassment. By viewing sexual bullying as harassment, school districts can take specific actions based on the federal definition of sexual harassment and the rights of students under Title IX. Several programs show promise in reducing sexual bullying and harassment in schools, including Expect Respect: A School-Based Program Promoting Safe and Healthy Relationships for Youth and Shifting Boundaries: Lessons on Relationships for Students in Middle School.

5

■ ■ ■

Under-the-Radar Bullying: Religious Bullying
and Bullying by Teachers

Do not condemn the judgment of another because it differs from
your own. You may both be wrong.

—Dandemis

While the destructive nature of peer-on-peer bullying in school has been
extensively reported in the literature, relatively little is known about the
prevalence and impact of bullying that often occurs "under the radar" in U.S.
public schools. This chapter explores two seldom discussed types of bullying in schools—students bullied for their religious beliefs (or nonbelief),
and students bullied by teachers and other adults in schools. It discusses the
nature and extent of religious bullying in U.S. public schools, its legal and
moral frameworks, and strategies for preventing religious bullying in schools.
It then moves to a discussion of bullying by teachers and other adults in
school, why there is a paucity of research and knowledge on teachers who
bully students, and the educational and emotional consequences for students
who are victims of teacher bullying. It concludes with recommendations for
increasing knowledge of teacher bullying and strategies for preventing this
form of bullying in schools.

What Is Religious Bullying?

Religious bullying has been defined as repeated acts of aggression in which
the power of institutional religion is used to mock, humiliate, or threaten
others who do not share the same religious beliefs or practices (Croucher
et al., 2009). The potential for bullying based on being "different" in terms

of one's religious beliefs (or "unaffiliated" with any religious tradition) is of particular concern in communities where there is a significant discrepancy between the religious affiliation (or nonaffiliation) of the majority compared with those of other religious traditions (or nonbelievers). For example, there is a potential for religious bullying by conservative Evangelical Christians within the "Bible Belt," by Mormons in Utah, by Catholics in several Northeastern states or even by those unaffiliated with any religious tradition in certain Northeastern states or certain Western states (The Pew Forum on Religion and Public Life, 2012).

What Are the Nature and Extent of Religious Bullying in U.S. Public Schools?

Few empirical studies have explored the extent of and impact of religious bullying in U.S. public schools. However, there is some evidence that remarks that mock or humiliate another student's religious beliefs may not be viewed as a form of bullying. For example, one study has reported that negative religious remarks were "less likely than other remarks to result in teacher intervention" (Harris Interactive and GLSEN, 2005, p. 36).

Only one empirical study on religious bullying could be located, and that study involved a survey of over 800 British school children. The authors of this study reported that one in four British young people who practice a religion have been bullied due to their faith or the wearing of religious symbols (Interfaith Report, 2008). For example, one 13-year-old student reported, "I am an atheist, so people were calling me the devil and the anti-Christ." A 14-year-old reported, "they were shouting 'Jews killed Jesus'. Some of them were my friends; they didn't know I was Jewish." A 15-year-old reported that he was bullied all the time because he stated, "I believe in Jesus and the Bible." This study of religious bullying among British students reported that victims had trouble sleeping, drank or took drugs, were constantly frightened, were stressed out, and were unable to concentrate at school (Interfaith Report, 2008).

While empirical research on religious bullying in U.S. schools has focused primarily on the bullying of LGBTQ students (see Chapter 4 of this volume for an in-depth discussion of LGBTQ bullying), a number of case studies and legal briefs suggest that religious bullying in U.S. public schools may be a much broader and more pervasive form of bullying than many currently acknowledge. For example, a straight-A, female student, whose family was pagan, was physically and emotionally bullied over several years in a rural area of East Tennessee. Reportedly, this female student was beaten and ridiculed by other students for not being a Christian, repeatedly called a "Satan worshipper" and "witch," accused of "eating babies," and called a "lesbian." Three boys who grabbed her by the back of the neck and told her that she should change her religion or they'd "change it for her" also chased her down the hallway. In addition, she was forced to attend regular Bible study classes during the school day, urged to lead the school and her class in prayer, sent to the principal's office for not attending a Christian tent revival during school hours, and also told by a teacher to "keep quiet because you'll get in trouble" after she wrote a paper about religious freedom (India Tracy Campaign, 2005). In another case, a 14-year-old girl in an Ohio school district was called a "dirty Jew" and told that she would "rot in hell" because she didn't believe in Jesus Christ (Higgins, 2011). In another case, a Muslim junior high school student was reportedly kicked so hard in the groin that he bled in his urine (Marcus, 2011).

Beyond these individual cases, there have also been reports of religious bullying in U.S. public schools that target groups of students based on their religious beliefs. For example, it has been reported that dozens of students at certain schools have carried out "Kick a Jew Day" on school grounds during school hours (Marcus, 2011) and that religious hectoring by students in a northern Virginia high school is very aggressive, with teenagers being verbally assaulted by students who "roam corridors demanding to know if their fellow students share their messianic religious visions—and if not, why not?" (Rodgers, 2009, para.7).

Beyond the obvious legal issues involving the separation of church and state, these incidents raise questions about the line between unwanted proselytizing and religious bullying. For example, an atheist student in a middle school in South Carolina was ordered, as punishment for forgetting his belt and his gym clothing, to copy religious essays proclaiming a belief in God and stating that he was thankful God would help him remember these items in the future (Eckholm, 2011a). In another case, at a high school near Pensacola, Fla., teachers cited the Bible as fact in class, and one teacher preached to students with a bullhorn as they arrived at school (Eckholm, 2011a). In another case in Tennessee, teachers led students in prayer and Bible study and allowed Gideons International to distribute Bibles during school hours (Eckholm, 2011a).

In an effort to learn more about the extent and nature of religious bullying in schools located within one area of the "Bible Belt," my research team and I recently facilitated a series of focus groups involving students who identify with minority religious traditions (e.g., Muslim, Jewish, Catholic, Unitarian Universalist) as well as those with no religious affiliation (e.g., atheist, agnostic). While we are in the process of analyzing our data for an in-depth research report, we have identified several themes and issues related to students' direct experiences with or witnessing of religious bullying in the public schools they attend (see Box 5.1).

Box 5.1 Themes and Issues Related to Students' Direct Experiences With or Witnessing of Religious Bullying in Public Schools in One Bible Belt Community

- Non-Christian students endure slurs, verbal bullying, and physical threats while at their public school. Examples include: "Heil Hitler!" (to a Jewish student), "What would you do if I punched you in the face until you said you were Christian?""Your beliefs are crazy, totally wacko," and "You're going to hell and I am going to send you there." Even Catholics heard slurs such as "Dirty Catholic," and several Catholic students were told that they were going to hell because they worshipped statues and worshipped Mary. One Catholicstudent commented that a teacher said "Catholics were not Christian" in front of the class.

- Religious holidays (e.g., Ramadan) and news stories (e.g., death of Osama bin Laden, Saddam Hussein) trigger bullying incidents. For example, a coach repeatedly taunted a Muslim student with food during Ramadan. (Ramadan is an Islamic holiday during which Muslims fast from sunrise to sunset, and not even water is to be consumed). Muslim students were also ridiculed after news/historical events (such as Saddam Hussein's death, Osama bin Laden's death, and 9/11 anniversaries), by being called "terrorists" and accused of being related to Saddam Hussein or Osama bin Laden.

- Some religious bullying in public schools begins with teacher comments or assignments in the classroom that appear to carry over to peer group interactions outside the classroom. In one instance, a religious history teacher asked if there were any Catholics in the class because this teacher did not want to offend any Catholics in the class in their class discussion of Catholicism. In another instance, a teacher asked a Muslim student to write an essay on Islam, and this Muslim student was the only student in that class who had to present her essay in front of the class.
- Students' clothing and diet that are part of one's religious beliefs can trigger bullying incidents. Muslim girls seemed to suffer most of the bullying due to wearing clothes with long sleeves, long pants or skirts year-round and the hijab headscarf.
- Catholic and Jewish students felt that they were welcome to attend Christian-sponsored student clubs and organizations at the public schools they attended.

Understanding Religious Bullying Through Legal and Moral Frameworks

Before we can begin to address religious bullying in schools, it is important to understand the broader context within which religious bullying occurs. The central legal issue facing school officials is balancing the rights of free speech (including religious expression) as well as protecting students from being coerced by others to accept certain religious (or antireligious) beliefs (American Civil Liberties Union, n.d.). This is a particular concern in communities where there is little religious diversity and the potential abuse of power by those who are in the religious majority must be constantly monitored. Legally, students have the right to pray in public schools either as individuals or in groups and, if it is not disruptive, students can also share their faith with other students and form afterschool religious clubs (ACLU, n.d.). The core issue here is differentiating between a respectful invitation to share one's religious beliefs versus an ongoing and unwelcome religious hectoring of students who have made it very clear that they do not share and do not wish to share another's religious beliefs. In other words, when does proselytizing cross the line and become religious bullying?

In addition to the legal issues involved, it is also important to recognize the "subtle and not-so subtle promotion of Christianity in public schooling and the institutional enforcement of dominant Christian standards in our schools which serves to dominate and subordinate non-Christians" (Blumenfeld, 2006, p. 195). This is a form of hegemony where Christian beliefs and standards are "taken for granted as common sense, and works to the power advantage of one group (the hegemonic one) and the disadvantage of others" (Hulsether, 2007, p. 10). Blumenfeld argues that there is an array of invisible, unearned, and largely unacknowledged benefits accorded to Christians in our public schools. For example, Christian students and school personnel "can be reasonably assured that when they talk about their religious traditions or wear religious symbols such as a cross, they will not be the targets of ridicule, discrimination, or harassment by their peers and school officials. Students and school personnel of other faith communities or non-believers have no such assurance" (pp. 204–205). This largely unacknowledged Christian hegemony in U.S. public schools can distort and complicate definitions and assessments of religious bullying.

Strategies for Preventing Religious Bullying in Schools

A number of recommendations for increasing religious tolerance in U.S. public schools have been developed by Blumenfeld (2006). These recommendations are highlighted in Box 5.2. As seen in Box 5.2, first and foremost, it is important to develop and offer ongoing training to all school personnel that focuses on the religious accommodation needs of students and school personnel. This ongoing training should include discussions of world religions, the history of religion, and religious oppression in the United States and other countries throughout the world. It is important that teachers become aware of how they can teach about religious tolerance and religious freedom and remain within the bounds of the Constitution. One helpful resource is a series of lesson plans designed to promote religious tolerance that have been developed for public school teachers by Teaching Tolerance (a project of the Southern Poverty Law Center). For more information, see http://www.tolerance.org/activity/understanding-other-religious-beliefs and http://www.tolerance.org/activity/understanding-religious-clothing.

All school personnel should also be encouraged to educate themselves about religious minorities and nonbelievers. It should be assumed that there are people of other faiths and nonbelievers in one's school, workplace, and

Box 5.2 Recommendations for Increasing Religious Tolerance in U.S. Public Schools

- Develop and implement ongoing in-service training for all school personnel that focuses on the needs, concerns, and life experiences of members of different faith communities and of nonbelievers.
- Organize and sponsor community-wide forums to discuss issues related to religious diversity and religious pluralism.
- Develop and implement school policies designed to protect students, faculty, staff, and administrators of every (and no) faith from harassment, bullying, and discrimination, and to provide equality of treatment.
- Materials in library collections, curriculum, and school programs regarding religious issues and world religions should include accurate, honest, up-to-date, and age-appropriate information presented uniformly and without bias or judgment.
- Recruit and hire faculty and staff from disparate religious and spiritual backgrounds as well as nonbelievers to serve as supportive role models for all youth.

Source: Adapted from Blumenfeld (2006).

community. Attempts should be made to experience major Christian holiday seasons from the perspective of non-Christians. Care should be taken to avoid imposing one's traditions and values on others. It is also helpful to attend cultural events of other religions.

Second, community-wide forums should be held that focus on becoming more aware of issues related to religious tolerance, religious diversity, and religious pluralism. One helpful resource is the Pluralism Project at Harvard University. According to information contained on their Web site, the mission of the Pluralism Project is: (a) to document and better understand the changing contours of American religious demography, focusing especially on those cities and towns where the new plurality has been most evident and discerning the ways in which this plurality is both visible and invisible in American public life; (b) to study the religious communities themselves—their temples, mosques, gurudwaras and retreat centers, their informal networks and emerging institutions, their forms of adaptation and religious education in the American context, their encounter with the other religious traditions of our common society, and their encounter with civic institutions; (c) to explore the ramifications and implications of America's new plurality through case studies of particular cities and towns, looking at the response of Christian and Jewish communities to their new neighbors; the development of interfaith councils and networks; the new theological and pastoral questions that emerge from the pluralistic context; and the recasting of traditional church–state issues in a wider context; and (d) to discern, in light of this work, the emerging meanings of religious "pluralism," both for religious communities and for public institutions, and to consider the real challenges and opportunities of a public commitment to pluralism in the light of the new religious contours of America. More information about the Pluralism Project at Harvard University can be found at http://pluralism.org/.

Third, it is important to develop school policies that protect students and school staff who hold minority religious beliefs from all forms of harassment and bullying. One helpful resource is the Policies & Procedures page at the First Amendment Schools (FAS) Web site. According to information contained on their Web site, this site offers thematic overviews, expert commentary, and sample policies for schools intent on adhering to the latest interpretations of First Amendment law and promoting the responsible usage of First Amendment freedoms. FAS was launched by the Association for Supervision and Curriculum Development (ASCD) and the First Amendment Center in 2001, and today the First Amendment Schools Network includes schools throughout the nation, both public and private, that are committed to becoming laboratories of democratic freedom. More information about First Amendment Schools can be found at their Web site: http://www. firstamendmentschools.org/about/aboutindex.aspx.

Fourth, up-to-date and age-appropriate materials pertaining to religious issues (e.g., collections of books, videos/DVDs) should be developed and maintained. When introducing controversial topics, such as Christian privilege and religious oppression, it is effective to bring a panel of outside speakers into the classroom that identify as Christian and understand the benefits they are accorded on the basis of their religious identity. Students are often more inclined to "hear" those who are most like them. It is also important to include members of other faith communities as well as nonbelievers on these panels.

Lastly, just as it is important for schools to hire racially and ethnically diverse faculty and staff to serve as role models and supports for all students, school officials should also recruit and hire faculty and staff who hold diverse religious and spiritual beliefs (as well as nonbelievers) to serve as role models and supports for students from minority religious traditions or who are nonbelievers.

Bullying by Teachers and Other Adults in School

It is essential to recognize bullying in all its forms in schools. While the vast majority of teachers interact respectfully with students, there is mounting anecdotal evidence that some teachers do indeed bully students. This is a potentially devastating type of bullying that is largely unacknowledged and often hidden from view. Although state laws protect minors from such physical and emotional abuse at the hands of parents or guardians (Child Welfare Information Gateway, 2011), these legal protections do not follow students into the school setting. Although the destructive nature of peer-on-peer bullying in school has been extensively reported in the literature (Borg, 1999; Boulton & Underwood, 1992; Olweus, 1993), relatively little attention, thus far, has focused on teachers as perpetrators of bullying. However, even if only a few teachers engage in this behavior within a school, the consequences are profound for the victims as well as the entire environment of the school (McEvoy, 2005).

Since a positive teacher–student relationship is such a critical factor in a child's development and educational experience, there is a pressing need to increase our understanding of this insidious form of bullying in our schools. As with other forms of bullying discussed throughout this volume, the abuse of power is also a central component of teacher bullying. For example, Twemlow & Fonagy (2005) define a teacher-bully as a teacher "*who uses his or her power* to punish, manipulate or disparage a student beyond what would be a reasonable disciplinary procedure (p. 2387)." McEvoy (2005) expands on this definition by defining teacher bullying as a "pattern of conduct, rooted in a *power differential*, that threatens, harms, humiliates, induces fear, or causes students substantial emotional distress...like peer-on-peer bullying, [teacher bullying] is an *abuse of power* that tends to be chronic and often is expressed in a public manner" (p. 1). Because of the vast power differential between teachers and students, teacher bullying often results in students having little or no ability to defend themselves (Hyman & Perone, 1998).

Why Is There a Paucity of Research on Teachers Who Bully Students?

There are several unique and highly political aspects to teacher bullying that make it much more difficult to assess and address. First, bullying behaviors by teachers are often equated with maintaining order and discipline and, therefore, often "undetectable." Teachers who bully students will often disguise their demeaning and cruel behavior as appropriate disciplinary responses to unacceptable student behavior or as a necessary means to "motivate" students to behave appropriately (McEvoy, 2005). Devine (1996) has pointed out the tough language, intimidation, tough demeanor, and tough posturing that some teachers use to exert their power and authority over students are often praised by other teachers and administrators.

Second, there are few if any negative consequences or any type of retribution for teachers who bully students (Koenig & Daniels, 2011). Current school policies do not even recognize teacher-to-student bullying as a problem and, consequently, fail to provide any formal mechanism to remedy student complaints against abusive teachers. This lack of policies and institutional inaction serve to tacitly sanction a teacher's bullying behavior and mistreatment of students (McEvoy, 2005; Sylvester, 2011). Moreover, parents may be reluctant to confront a teacher due to feelings of intimidation, or they may be from a culture where teaching is held in high esteem and a teacher's conduct or classroom management techniques would never be questioned (Sylvester, 2011).

Third, conducting research on teacher-on-student bullying is difficult because researchers cannot simply observe this phenomenon because teachers are likely to modify their behavior in the presence of observers (Hyman et al., 1997), and teachers may be reluctant to discuss this problem openly out of fear of being shunned by their colleagues (Twemlow, Fonagy, & Sacco, 2004).

Fourth, if a teacher is accused of bullying a student, a labor conflict with teacher unions can ensue where the protection of the bullying teacher can take precedence over the impact that the bullying teacher has on the larger body of teachers or the student victims of teacher bullies (Twemlow, Fonagy, Sacco, & Brethour, 2006).

What We Currently Know About Teacher Bullying in Schools

Several researchers have begun to systematically investigate teachers who bully students. For example, McEvoy (2005) reported that in many schools at least one or more teachers can be identified as abusive toward students and that teachers who bully tend to be established and secure in their positions. Twemlow & Fonagy (2005) found that 45% of teachers in their study stated they had bullied a student at some point in their teaching career and that teachers who bully students may contribute to students' behavioral problems in school. In another study, 70% of elementary teachers admitted to bullying students on an isolated basis, and 18% of elementary teachers reported bullying students on a frequent basis (Twemlow, Fonagy, Sacco, & Brethour, 2006).

I was the coauthor of a study that explored the extent to which students in an alternative school reported being victimized by teachers or other adults during their school career (Whitted & Dupper, 2008). Participants in this study were a convenience sample of 50 students ranging in age from 11 to 18 years old who attended alternative schools in an urban school district in a Southeastern state in the United States during the 2004–2005 school year. To determine if students were physically or psychologically victimized by peers or adults at some point during their school career and the nature and the frequency of this victimization, participants were asked to complete a revised version of the Student Alienation and Trauma Survey (Hyman & Snook, 2002). We found that 86% of the respondents reported at least one incident of adult physical maltreatment in school, and 88% reported at least one incident of adult psychological maltreatment in school. The most commonly reported types of physical maltreatment in our study involved an adult not allowing them to go to the bathroom (70%); an adult grabbing them very hard (38%); and adults punching them (32%), pushing them (28%), or shaking them (26%). The most commonly reported types of psychological maltreatment involved being yelled at by an adult (66%), having an adult make them stay away from others (64%), and being ignored by an adult (56%). Students reported that adults made fun of them or teased them in a harmful way (34%), said mean things about students' family (34%), or made fun of them because of their race or color of their skin (20%). Students who are victimized by adults in schools are involved in a power imbalance that makes them extremely vulnerable to ongoing mistreatment and abuse. Being "pushed by an adult into a snack machine" or being told by an adult that you "dress like a whore" is humiliating enough, but in not being able to defend yourself against such hurtful or demeaning comments, you are further victimized. For example, when a student attempts to defend himself or herself in response to a demeaning comment from a teacher or other adult, the student is often also punished by "receiving a detention or being suspended from school for being 'disrespectful' toward an adult in authority" (p. 339). We conclude by stating that the "results of this study suggest that teacher-on-student bullying may be more ubiquitous than previously thought" (p. 339).

The Educational and Emotional Consequences for Students Who Are Victims of Teacher Bullying

The impact of teacher bullying can be more devastating and developmentally destructive than peer bullying due to the considerable power differential between adults and students (McEvoy, 2005). Students who feel ridiculed, mistreated, verbally or physically attacked, and/or ignored by the school staff can develop feelings of victimization and alienation, potentially resulting in a range of problems, from lags in emotional and intellectual development, to behavioral, social, emotional, and academic problems, to attempted suicide (Hyman, 1990; Hyman et al., 1997; Hyman, Zelikoff, & Clarke, 1988; Vargas-Moll, 1991; Zelikoff, 1990). Hyman and Perone (1998) state that adult-to-student maltreatment may result in students developing symptoms of posttraumatic stress disorder.

The potentially destructive nature of teacher-on-student bullying is powerfully described by McEvoy (2005):

> Like stalking victims, students who are the targets of teachers who bully feel trapped in a situation where the abuser is all-powerful. Sometimes they may be literally trapped in an environment (e.g., classroom or office) where offensive conduct is imposed upon them and there is no escape. More often, they feel situationally trapped and bereft of a way to mitigate this harmful situation. Any complaint about the abusive behavior places the student at risk of retaliation by the teacher, including the use of grades as a sanction. Equally important, it is the student not the teacher who suffers deprivations if he or she misses class, withdraws from a course, or has to avoid certain classes because the teacher is a bully. (p. 3)

Recommendations for Increasing Our Knowledge of and Preventing Teacher Bullying in Schools

Based on what we currently know, and more importantly, what we don't know about teachers who bully students, we need to take several steps to increase our understanding of and knowledge of teacher bullying. First and foremost, permission needs to be granted to researchers who want to examine this type of bullying in schools (Twemlow et al., 2006). There is a pressing need to explicitly define teacher bullying, and to accurately assess how often it occurs, how it is manifested, and its short- and long-term impact on students' development and school experiences. We also need national data on teachers who bully. Currently, the Indicators of School Crime and Safety annual survey, the most definitive assessment of safety in schools, does not include survey questions on teachers who bully students (although there are statistics on students who bully teachers) (Koenig & Daniels, 2011).

Second, teachers need to be trained in effective classroom management techniques built upon the establishment of positive teacher–student relationships. It is important for teachers to be able to distinguish between reasonable and effective disciplinary techniques as opposed to discipline that relies upon fear and intimidation. Some teachers believe that they must be punitive to be effective disciplinarians. However, "tough discipline" techniques based on intimidation and fear (e.g., screaming at students, using sarcasm, threats, or ridicule, or publicly humiliating students) often cross over the line into bullying (McEvoy, 2005). I discuss a relationship-based, preventive model of school discipline (Dupper, 2010) where students "behave appropriately, not out of fear of punishment or desire for reward, but out of a sense of personal responsibility, respect, and regard for the group" (Woolfolk Hoy & Weinstein, 2006, p. 210). It is a discipline model that: (a) is built upon caring and trust, and dignity and cooperation, and that communicates to all students that they are respected and valued members of the school community (Belenardo, 2001; Freiberg & Lapointe, 2006); (b) views discipline as "teachable moments" that provide students with an opportunity for learning and growth (Sullivan & Keeney, 2008); (c) is preventive in nature and anticipates the inevitable conflicts that occur on a daily basis in schools and implements strategies designed to defuse rather than escalate these interpersonal conflicts; (d) utilizes social learning theory to teach social, behavioral, and cognitive skills to children and youth using structured skill-training techniques and lesson plans (Jenson, 2006).

Third, because of the considerable power differential between teachers and students, teachers must be held to a high level of accountability for their behavior toward students (Koenig & Daniels, 2011). While teachers have every right to maintain order and discipline, they also have the responsibility to present themselves as models of the kind of behavior they expect from their students (McEvoy, 2005). Students should be constantly reassured that they are valued as individuals (Parsons, 2005). Sarcasm or demeaning comments have no place within the classroom (Sylvester, 2011). Several recent news stories have reported on students' videotaping of bullying incidents with teachers with their cell phones and then turning the videotape over to school authorities. The question must be asked, "Is a cell phone videotape a student's only means of catching teachers and holding them accountable for their bullying behavior"? Lastly, students need to learn how to respond to teacher bullying (Sylvester, 2011). For example, procedures need to be established that include the anonymous reporting of teacher bullying.

Summary

Religious bullying has been defined as repeated acts of aggression in which the power of institutional religion is used to mock, humiliate, or threaten others who do not share the same religious beliefs or practices. The potential for bullying based on being "different" in terms of one's religious beliefs (or being unaffiliated with any religious tradition) is of particular concern in communities where there is a significant discrepancy between the religious affiliation of the majority compared with those of other religious traditions (or nonbelievers). The authors of a study of religious bullying that involved a survey of over eight hundred British school children reported that one in four British young people who practice a religion have been bullied due to their faith or the wearing of religious symbols. While I was unable to locate any empirical studies that focused on religious bullying in U.S. public schools, a number of case studies and legal briefs suggest that religious bullying in U.S. public schools may be a much broader and more pervasive form of bullying than many currently acknowledge.

The central legal issue facing school officials is balancing the rights of free speech (including religious expression) as well as protecting students from being coerced by others to accept certain religious (or antireligious) beliefs. In essence, there is a need to differentiate a respectful invitation to share one's religious beliefs from an ongoing and unwelcome religious hectoring of students who have made it very clear that they do not share and do not wish to share another's religious beliefs. In other words, when does proselytizing cross the line and become religious bullying? Christian hegemony in U.S. public schools can also distort and complicate definitions and assessments of religious bullying.

Recommendations for increasing religious tolerance in U.S. public schools include (a) ongoing training to all school personnel that focuses on the religious accommodation needs of students and school personnel; (b) holding community-wide forums that focus on becoming more aware of issues related to religious tolerance, religious diversity, and religious pluralism;

(c) the development of school policies that protect students and school staff who hold minority religious beliefs from all forms of harassment and bullying; (d) the development and maintenance of up-to-date and age-appropriate materials pertaining to religious issues; and (e) the recruitment and hiring of faculty and staff who hold diverse religious and spiritual beliefs (as well as nonbelievers) to serve as role models and supports for students from minority religious traditions or who are nonbelievers.

While the vast majority of teachers interact respectfully with students, there are anecdotal evidence and some preliminary studies focusing on a form of bullying in schools that is largely unacknowledged and often hidden from view—teachers who bully students. Since a positive teacher–student relationship is such a critical factor in a child's development and educational experience, there is a pressing need to increase our understanding of this insidious form of bullying in our schools. A teacher-bully is a teacher who uses his or her power to punish, manipulate, or disparage a student beyond what would be a reasonable disciplinary procedure. Because of the vast power differential between teachers and students, teacher bullying often results in students having little or no ability to defend themselves.

Teacher bullying is difficult to assess and address because bullying behaviors are often equated with maintaining order and discipline and are often "undetectable." Current school policies do not even recognize teacher-to-student bullying as a problem and, consequently, fail to provide any formal mechanism to remedy student complaints against abusive teachers. Conducting research on teacher-on-student bullying is difficult because teachers are likely to modify their behavior in the presence of observers, and teachers may be reluctant to discuss this problem openly out of fear of being shunned by their colleagues. Teacher unions also often protect the bullying teacher. One of the few studies of teacher bullying reported that 45% of teachers stated they had bullied a student at some point in their teaching career while another study found that 70% of elementary teachers admitted to bullying students on an isolated basis and 18% of elementary teachers reported bullying students on a frequent basis. A study I coauthored found that 86% of the respondents reported at least one incident of adult physical maltreatment in school and 88% reported at least one incident of adult psychological maltreatment in school.

The impact of teacher bullying can be more devastating and developmentally destructive than peer bullying due to the considerable power differential between adults and students. We need to take several steps to increase our understanding and knowledge of teacher bullying, including explicitly defining it, and accurately assessing how often it occurs, how it is manifested, and its short- and long-term impact on students' development and school experiences. Teachers also need to be trained in effective classroom management techniques built upon the establishment of positive teacher–student relationships.

6

███

Best Practices in Preventing School Bullying: A Whole-School Approach and Beyond

> What this world needs is a new kind of army—the army of the kind.
>
> —*Cleveland Amory*

This final chapter begins by discussing strategies that do not work in combating bullying. It then describes the philosophy and key features of a whole-school approach as a framework for developing and implementing comprehensive bullying prevention and intervention strategies, including a detailed discussion of school-level, classroom-level, and student-level components. It describes several empirically supported bullying prevention programs that are based on a whole-school approach and strategies for integrating bullying prevention strategies into Schoolwide Positive Behavior Support (SWPBS). It describes several innovative approaches designed to combat bullying and concludes with a discussion of tough antibullying laws across the United States, issues related to state bullying policies, and combating bullying as a human rights issue.

What Strategies Do Not Work in Combating Bullying?

Because bullying differs from other kinds of violence, it does not lend itself to the same interventions that may be effective in addressing other types of peer conflict. As stated throughout this volume, bullying involves powerful students against students who are less powerful, rather than a conflict between peers of relatively equal status. Moreover, bullying behavior does not result from a deficit in social skills. As a consequence, conflict resolution, peer mediation

---

strategies, and group therapy focusing on increasing self-esteem have all been shown to be relatively ineffective with bullies (Limber & Nation, 1998. In fact, interventions that involve peers, such as using students as peer mediators, have been shown to be associated with *increases* in victimization (Farrington and Ttofi, 2010). Peer influences can be a constructive or destructive force on bullying and need to be handled with knowledge, skill, and care (Rodkin, 2011; Vaillancourt, McDougall, Hymel, & Sunderani, 2010). Zero tolerance discipline that involves an escalating series of sanctions if rules are broken also appear to be ineffective because it simply reinforces a bully's "intrinsic belief that power and aggression are the essential and controlling values in a society" (Parsons, 2005, pp. 66–67).

A Whole-School Approach to Bullying Prevention

Two decades of research have produced general agreement among researchers that narrowly conceived, piecemeal, add-on strategies have not been shown to be effective in combating bullying in schools (Ttofi & Farrington, 2009; Vreeman & Carroll, 2007; UCLA Center for Mental Health Services in Schools, 2011, p. 7). However, bullying can be reduced substantially by implementing a comprehensive, whole-school approach that modifies all levels of the social ecology of the school (i.e., individual, classroom, school, and community levels) (Blosnich & Bossarte, 2011; Holt, Keyes, & Koening, 2011; Olweus & Limber, 2010; Srabstein & Leventhal, 2010; Swearer, Espelage, Vaillancourt, & Hymel, 2010).

School-Level Components

Based on research findings and best practices, Table 6.1 lists nine essential school-level components to combat bullying, within a whole-school approach. All of these nine strategies are important in changing the culture and climate of the school—an essential element of a whole-school approach. I will describe each of these nine components in detail here.

An essential first step is conducting an accurate assessment of the extent and nature of bullying in the school. Adults are not always good at estimating the nature and extent of bullying at their school and are often surprised by the amount of bullying in their school, the types of bullying that are most common, or the places where bullying occurs most often (U.S. Department of Health and Human Services, n.d.,a). As a result, it is often useful to assess bullying by administering an anonymous questionnaire to students about bullying. An anonymous questionnaire should be completed by students to

Table 6.1 A Whole-School Approach to Combat Bullying: Essential Components and Best Practices

---

School-Level Components: Strategies for Changing the Culture and Climate of the School

---

1. Assess the extent and nature of bullying.
2. Obtain the support, buy-in, and commitment of all key stakeholders.
3. A school coordinating team should be formed.
4. In-service training for teachers and other school staff.
5. The language and needs of youth should be taken into account.
6. Shift the power dynamics and change the social norms in schools by empowering bystanders.
7. Establish and enforce policies related to bullying that include expectations for behavior.
8. Increase adult supervision in areas where bullying occurs most frequently.
9. Middle school years are critical.

Classroom-Level Components: Strategies Involving Teachers and Other Adults in the School

---

1. Regular classroom meetings should be held by teachers to discuss issues related to bullying.
2. Antibullying themes and messages should be integrated into the curriculum.
3. Teachers should encourage the reporting of bullying incidents.
4. All school personnel should model positive interpersonal skills.

Student-Level Components: Strategies Designed to Help Victims, Bullies, and Bystanders

---

1. All staff should be equipped to intervene consistently and appropriately in all bullying situations.
2. Designated staff should hold sensitive follow-up meetings with children who are bullied and (separately) with children who bully.
3. Students should learn skills to intervene and provide assistance to bullying victims.

Note. *Sources:* Blosnich & Bossarte, 2011; Boyd & Marwick, 2011; Coivin, Tobin, Beard, Hadan, & Sprague, 1998; Espelage, 2004; Frey et al., 2011; Graham, 2009; Greene, 2006; Kallestad & Olweus, 2003; Low et al., 2011; Northwest Regional Educational Laboratory, 2001; Olweus et al., 1999; Olweus & Limber, 2010; Parent Teacher Association of Connecticut, Inc., 2000; Parsons, 2005;Rigby, 1995; Rodkin, 2011; Swearer & Doll, 2001; Swearer & Espelage, 2011; Srabstein & Leventhal, 2010; UCLA Center for Mental Health Services in Schools, 2011.

assess the extent and nature of bullying at individual schools. Findings from this survey can be used to motivate adults to take action against bullying and to help administrators and other educators tailor a bullying prevention strategy to the particular needs of the school. Data from this survey can also serve as a baseline from which administrators and other educators can measure their progress in reducing bullying over time (U.S. Department of Health and Human Services, n.d.,a). A recent compendium published by the Centers for Disease Control and Prevention entitled *Measuring Bullying Victimization, Perpetration, and Bystander Experiences: A Compendium of Assessment Tools* provides tools to measure a range of bullying experiences, including bully perpetration, bully victimization, bully-victim experiences, and bystander experiences. Parsons (2005) also offers a series of questions designed to assess the current state of a school's antibullying environment, including "Does your school staff insist on an environment completely free of sexist, racial, cultural, ability-related, and homophobic stereotyping?," "Do all teachers display a respectful attitude toward all students and a genuine regard for their learning?," "Do all teachers in the school use cooperative learning strategies?," "Are teachers meaningfully involved in the decision-making and problem-solving processes on a school-wide basis?" (p. 68).

A second step involves garnering the widespread support and significant commitment of all key stakeholders (e.g., administrators, teachers, students, parents, auxiliary school staff, and community partners) in recognizing the importance of the problem and making a commitment to establish prevention and intervention programs and policies (Low et al., 2011; Olweus, Limber, & Mihalic, 1999). There should be no "end date" for bullying prevention activities (Low et al., 2011; U.S. Department of Health and Human Services, n.d.,a).

A third step is the formation of a school coordinating team. This team includes representatives from a number of groups, including a school administrator, a teacher from each grade, a member of the nonteaching staff, a school counselor or other school-based mental health professional (e.g., school social worker), a school nurse, and a parent. This team is involved in the development, implementation, maintenance, and evaluation of the program (U.S. Department of Health and Human Services, n.d.,a). A school coordinating team should meet regularly to develop bullying prevention rules, policies, and activities; motivate staff, students, and parents; and ensure that the efforts continue over time. A student advisory group can also be formed to focus on bullying prevention strategies and provide valuable suggestions and feedback to adults (e.g., student input in developing rules against bullying) (U.S. Department of Health and Human Services, n.d.,a).

A fourth step involves the development and provision of ongoing in-service training for teachers and all adults in the school environment who interact with students (e.g., counselors, media specialists, school resource officers, nurses, lunchroom and recess aides, bus drivers, parent volunteers, custodians, cafeteria workers, maintenance staff, paraprofessionals, and secretaries) (U.S. Department of Health and Human Services, n.d.,a). Teachers are central figures in schools' efforts to intervene effectively and limit the negative effects of school bullying (Blosnich & Bossarte, 2011; Kallestad & Olweus, 2003). The critical importance of ongoing teacher training is evidenced by the findings that teachers often do not recognize more subtle forms of bullying (e.g., social exclusion, spreading rumors, and name-calling) and are less likely to intervene or know how to respond to bullying without specific training (Allen, 2010; Doll, Song, Champion, & Jones, 2011; Greene, 2006). This annual, in-service training should include recent research on the nature of bullying and its effects, how to use evidence-based strategies to help prevent bullying from occurring, and strategies for responding to bullying incidents (e.g., how to better understand and manage student social dynamics and strategies for handling aggression), as well as how to work with others at the school to help prevent bullying from occurring (U.S. Department of Health and Human Services, n.d.,a). Ongoing professional development should be provided for new employees who are hired after the start of the school year.

A fifth strategy recognizes that antibullying efforts cannot be successful unless the language and needs of youth are taken into account. Based on their interviews with and observations of youth over several years, Boyd & Marwick (2011) found that many youths engaged in practices that adults label "bullying" but that the youths do not name them as such because admitting that they're being bullied (or worse, that they are bullies) makes them feel weak and childish. Antibullying efforts cannot be successful if they make teenagers feel victimized without providing them the support to go from a position of victimization to one of empowerment. When teenagers acknowledge that they're being bullied, adults need to provide programs similar to those that help victims of abuse and recognize that emotional recovery can be a long and difficult process. The key is to help young people feel independently strong, confident, and capable without first requiring them to see themselves as either a victim or a perpetrator (Boyd & Marwick, 2011).

A sixth strategy focuses on shifting peer group norms and dynamics in schools by targeting bystanders in antibullying interventions. We have come to recognize that peer group dynamics and peer group norms play a critical role in fueling bullying incidents (Salmivalli, Voeten, & Poskiparta, 2011). Many bullying prevention programs have yielded less-than-encouraging outcomes because of their failure to address the fact that bullying might be a peer group norm (Swearer, Espelage, & Napolitano, 2009), and unless and until these peer group norms are modified, bullying behaviors will not decrease in our schools (Vaillancourt, Hymel, & McDougall, 2003). Peer group norms can be changed by capitalizing on the "power that peers have to disapprove of bullying" (Juvonen & Graham, 2004, p. 235) and changing the ways in which peers respond to bullying incidents that they witness (Frey et al., 2010; Orpinas & Horne, 2006; Salmivalli, Kärnä, & Poskiparta, 2010). In many schools, there are peer group norms that support bullying or reinforce the high social standing of bullies (Juvonen & Graham, 2004). Withdrawing bystander reinforcement (especially for high-status bullies) is a pathway for reducing bullying (Frey, Carlson Jones, Hirschstein, & Edstrom, 2011). Bystanders and witnesses to bullying must be empowered to act on behalf of the victim. For example, it must become "uncool" to bully, "cool" to help students who are bullied, and normative for staff and students to notice when a child is bullied or left out (U.S. Department of Health and Human Services, n.d.,a). By taking these steps, bullying becomes viewed as a problem for which everyone is responsible and in which there is no such thing as an innocent bystander. In essence, bullying becomes "socially unacceptable" (Farrington & Ttofi, 2010). There is evidence to suggest that bystanders who *do* intervene on behalf of the victim are typically students with high social status (e.g., Salmivalli, Lagerpetz, Bjorkqvist, Osterman, & Kaukiainen, 1996). Consequently, high-status peers are more likely to be successful in intervening on the part of the victim and "should be targeted in school-based intervention efforts" (Vaillancourt et al., 2003, p. 172). It is also important to note that positive bystander responses in bullying situations may be more effective with younger, elementary students than with older students because "younger students are significantly more likely to take direct positive action as bystanders (e.g., direct intervention, helping the victim, talking to adults) and that passive (do nothing) and aggressive (get back at the bully) responses increase with age" (Swearer et al., 2010, p. 40). Twemlow & Sacco (2007) have developed an intervention that is designed to alter these peer group dynamics by empowering helpful, natural leaders whom they refer to as *helpful bystanders.* These helpful bystanders foster wide support for kindness and helpfulness as "values with a higher social status, rather than the macho power of the bully dynamic. The helpfulness ideal was reinforced and the bullies and purveyors of prejudice were marginalized, to everyone's benefit" (Twemlow & Sacco, 2007, p. 244). Another promising program that takes advantage of peer relationships to combat bullying is the Finnish program *KiVa* (Salmivalli et al., 2010), *KiVa* has a strong emphasis on influencing onlookers to support the victim rather than encourage the bully. Several programs that empower peers to combat bullying are described in Box 6.1.

Box 6.1 Programs That Empower Peers to Combat Bullying

You Have the Power! (YHTP!)

The You Have the Power! (YHTP!) program was developed in Montgomery County, Md., in 2004 by Project Change teen members who wanted to take action to reduce bullying among students in their community. Project Change is a youth/adult partnership organization dedicated to promoting opportunities for youth to be engaged in, contribute to, and be satisfied members of their community. The YHTP! program features teen mentors working with middle and elementary students after school to raise awareness about characteristics, risks, and consequences of bullying. Teen mentors help younger kids learn about bullying prevention and develop a project to bring this valuable information to their schoolmates. YHTP! has been implemented at middle and elementary schools in Montgomery County, Md. Detailed information about the You Have the Power! program is available at: http://www.projectchange-md.org/yhtp/index.php.

Safe School Ambassadors (SSA)

The Safe School Ambassadors (SSA) program equips young people with nonviolent communication skills to speak up; intervene; and stop harassment, meanness, and all forms of bullying. Students acquire skills they can use in the moment, with their friends, to defuse and deescalate potentially hurtful incidents. Key adults are trained to facilitate regular small-group meetings of Ambassadors, which sharpen their skills, sustain their commitment, and increase their reporting of dangerous activities like planned fights or weapons on campus. Safe

---

School Ambassadors (SSA) is designed for students in the 4th–12th grades and has been implemented in 900 schools across 28 states and two Canadian provinces. The schools that have utilized the SSA program have seen results including decreased discipline referrals, suspensions, and expulsions; decreased tension and increased tolerance; increased flow of information to adults about potentially hurtful and violent acts; and improved school climate impacting attendance and academic performance. Detailed information about the Safe School Ambassadors is available at: http://www.community-matters.org/safe-school-ambassadors/.

Defeat the Label (DTL)

This new antibullying initiative is designed to empower teens to stand up to bullying and social labeling and to promote an inclusive, judgment-free society, void of social labels and stereotypes. To date, 1,300 teenagers around the world have signed up at DefeatTheLabel.com, where they record the results of weekly missions to do one specific act of good for a friend. Their Web site (http://defeatthelabel.com/) contains information about their in-school programs and a number of social advocacy tools.

Acknowledge, Care and Tell (ACT) Program

The Acknowledge, Care and Tell (ACT) Program is being implemented in the West Hartford, Conn., school district. The ACT Program educates students and parents on how to deal with bullying through the teaching of proactive prevention strategies. The focus of the program is to teach kids to be an ally to bullying victims. The assistant superintendent of West Hartford schools stated that this program stresses the importance of not being a bystander and being proactive and that "telling a parent or a trusted adult is the most important thing that you can do" (Gore-Oleksiw, 2011, para. 4).

Link-Crew

Link-crew is another student-initiated program in several West Hartford, Conn., high schools where upper classmen try to educate 8th graders, freshmen, and sophomores through assemblies and "step-up" programs within the transitioning grades. Link-crew will bring incoming freshman into the high school for a 2-day period to help build connections with juniors and seniors before school starts. The principal of one of the high schools stated that Link-crew "reduces the sense of alienation and reduces bullying and harassment" (Gore-Oleksiw, 2011, para. 26). As part of this program, one of the high schools will also implement "Stand up Against Bullying Week" and allow students to sell motivational bracelets and sign pledges to not bully (Gore-Oleksiw).

"Put-Ups" Program

In this West Hartford, Conn., program, a school, with the help of parents, selects peer leaders and puts them through weeks of training. These peer leaders then send out invitations to pizza and game parties to those students who are "loners" and struggling socially (Gore-Oleksiw, 2011).

A seventh strategy is the establishment and enforcement of a discipline policy that includes simple, clear rules about bullying as well as the development of appropriate positive and negative consequences that are consistently enforced. Although many school behavior codes implicitly forbid bullying, many codes do not explicitly state expectations for student behavior (U.S. Department of Health and Human Services, n.d.,a). The ultimate goal is to ensure that students are aware of adults' expectations that they refrain from bullying as well as help students who are bullied. It is important to make clear that the school not only expects students not to bully, but that it also expects them to be good citizens, not passive bystanders (U.S. Department of Health and Human Services, n.d.,a). For example, the Olweus Bullying Prevention Program (OBPD) (described later in this chapter) recommends that schools adopt four straightforward rules about bullying: (1) We will not bully others; (2) we will try to help students who are bullied; (3) we will make it a point to include students who are easily left out; and (4) if we know that someone is being bullied, we will tell an adult at school and an adult at home. Rigby (2002) recommends that a school's antibullying policy include a succinct *definition* of bullying with illustrations; a declaration of the *rights* of individuals in the school community—students, teachers, other, workers and parents—to be free of bullying and (if bullied) to be provided with help and support; a statement of *responsibilities* of members of the school community to abstain personally from bullying others in any way, and of those who witness it, to actively seek to stop bullying when it occurs and to give support to those who are victimized.

An eighth strategy involves an increase in adult supervision in the areas of the school where bullying occurs with the greatest frequency (i.e., "hot spots"). Bullying tends to thrive in locations where adults are not present or are not vigilant (U.S. Department of Health and Human Services, n.d.,a). Once school personnel have identified these "hot spots," they should discuss and implement creative ways to increase adults' presence in these locations in order to reduce opportunities for bullying. This strategy is important since it has been shown that having adults in hallways results in significant reductions in being physically bullied, having property vandalized, or having rumors spread (Blosnich & Bossarte, 2011).

A ninth and final strategy is to direct prevention and intervention efforts at the transition from elementary to middle school and throughout the critical middle school years due to a documented increase in bullying during early adolescence (Espelage, 2004).

Classroom-Level Components

Table 6.1 also lists four essential strategies to combat bullying at the classroom level. Regular classroom meetings to discuss issues related to bullying are essential. Teachers, with the support of administrators, should set aside 20–30 minutes each week (or every other week) to discuss bullying and peer relations with students. These classroom meetings help teachers to keep their fingers on the pulse of students' concerns, allow time for candid discussions about bullying and the harm that it can cause, and provide tools for students to address bullying problems (U.S. Department of Health and Human Services, n.d.,a). For example, teachers can help students acquire and practice positive behaviors with their peers through a strategy referred to as *empathy scaffolding*, which refers to the assistance offered by the teacher to help students acquire and practice positive behavior with peers. Empathy scaffolding "appears to be an important classroom strategy for teachers" (Frey et al., 2011, p. 273). Classroom meetings can also help teachers understand students' relationships at the school. For example, these meetings can be used to discuss which students are perceived to be popular and unpopular, whom students hang out with, who their friends are, and whom they dislike. These meetings can be used to identify and connect with students who have no friends and to identify student leaders who can encourage peers to stand up against bullying.

A second classroom-level strategy is the integration and incorporation of antibullying themes and messages throughout the school curriculum. For example, a school's curriculum can teach students how to achieve their goals by being assertive rather than aggressive and how to resolve conflicts with civility (U.S. Department of Health and Human Services, n.d.,a).

A third strategy involves implementing steps in schools to make it easier for students to come to a teacher to talk about bullying incidents. This can be accomplished by establishing anonymous reporting procedures for peer witnesses and assuring these peer witnesses that teachers and other adults will take appropriate action to address the situation. Strategies that foster positive bystander responses in bullying situations should also be developed and implemented.

A fourth classroom-level strategy involves the modeling of positive interpersonal skills by adults in the school. Students learn how to behave by observing the behavior of adults around them. If schools want to reduce bullying incidents, it is important that teachers and other adults model appropriate and respectful behavior toward students (e.g., teachers should not exhibit dominating or authoritarian behavior with students).

Student-Level Components

A whole-school approach to bullying prevention extends beyond primary prevention to include targeted one-on-one mental health treatment for bullies, victims, and bully-victims (Swearer & Espelage, 2011). Table 6.1 also lists four essential student-level strategies.

First, teachers and other school staff should consistently enforce nonpunitive, graduated consequences for bullying behaviors. Teachers and other adults should send clear messages that bullying will not be tolerated, and they should be equipped to intervene consistently and appropriately in all bullying situations. Specifically, all school staff should be able to intervene to stop bullying usually in the 1–2 minutes that one frequently has to deal with bullying incidents (U.S. Department of Health and Human Services, n.d.,a).

Second, it is also important that designated staff hold sensitive follow-up meetings with children who are bullied and separate meetings with children who bully. All adults in the school should protect and support bullying victims. Mental health professionals, such as school social workers, should provide supportive counseling to the bullying victim as well as protection from retaliation. Parents should also be encouraged to contact the school if they suspect their child is being bullied. In working with victims of bullying and their parents, it is important to remember that the typical victim has been threatened with more bullying if he or she "tattles." Fear from such threats causes many victims to decide to suffer quietly, and they ask their parents not to contact the school (Olweus, 1993). The primary response in dealing with bullies and their parents is to talk with bullies individually and tell them in absolute terms that bullying will not be tolerated and that it will end. Remedial measures designed to correct the bullying behavior and prevent another occurrence are important. This can be accomplished by teaching bullies replacement behaviors, empathy, tolerance, and sensitivity to diversity. Staff should also involve parents of students who bully whenever possible. Mental health resources should be made available to those students who are unable to stop bullying behaviors in spite of school intervention.

As a final step, all students should learn skills to intervene and provide assistance to bullying victims. For example, bystanders should be taught specific skills to intervene to help students who are being bullied, and these prosocial behaviors should be immediately reinforced.

Bullying Prevention Programs Based on a Whole-School Approach

There are several empirically supported bullying prevention programs based on a whole-school, comprehensive approach. Box 6.2 contains detailed information about three of these programs. The first and best known is the Olweus Bullying Prevention Program (OBPP). Implemented in Norway and Sweden in the early 1980s, the OBPP has as its major goal the reduction of victim/bullying problems among primary and secondary school children (Olweus, 1993). These goals are achieved through a restructuring of the school environment designed to reduce opportunities and rewards for engaging in bullying and to build a sense of community among students and adults within the school (Olweus, 1993, 2001; Olweus et al., 2007). The OBPP is based on the following four key principles: (1) adults should show warmth and positive interest in their students; (2) adults should set firm limits to unacceptable behavior; (3) adults should use consistent nonphysical, negative consequences when rules are broken; and (4) adults should function as authorities and positive role models (Olweus, 1993, 2001; Olweus et al., 2007). Although these principles and the components of the OBPP have remained largely unchanged, "ongoing research and experience

The Olweus Bullying Prevention Program (OBBP)

Bullying Prevention Program is a comprehensive, schoolwide program that targets students in elementary, middle, or junior high schools. Its goals are to reduce and prevent bullying problems among schoolchildren and to improve peer relations. The program is designed to be implemented at the school level, the class level, and the individual level. Schoolwide components include a questionnaire to assess the nature and prevalence of bullying at each school, and a school conference day to discuss bullying, plan interventions, and form a coordinating committee. Classroom components include the establishment and enforcement of class rules against bullying and regular class meetings with students. Individual components include interventions with children identified as bullies and victims and discussions with parents of involved students. The program has been found to reduce bullying among children, improve the social climate of classrooms, and reduce antisocial behaviors. Observational techniques showed marked decreases in relational and physical bullying. More information about this program is available at the Center for the Study and Prevention of Violence, University of Colorado, Web site at: http://www.colorado.edu/cspv/blueprints/modelprograms/BPP.html.

Bully-Proofing Your School (BPYS)

Bully-Proofing Your School (BPYS) is a nationally recognized school safety program, implemented in school districts throughout the United States and Canada, with a scientifically proven track record since its inception in 1994. Bully-Proofing Your School is a comprehensive program for handling bully/victim problems through the creation of a "caring majority" of students who take the lead in establishing and maintaining a safe and caring school community. The program focuses on converting the silent majority of students into a caring majority by teaching strategies that help them to avoid victimization and to take a stand for a bully-free school. In schools that have implemented the program, incidences of bullying behaviors have declined and feelings of safety among the students have increased. More information about this program is available at the National Center for School Engagement Web site at: http://www.schoolengagement.org/index.cfm/Bully%20 Proof%20Your%20School.

Steps to Respect

Steps to Respect is a multidimensional program that targets interventions at the individual, classroom, and school levels. The student curriculum teaches children the "three Rs" of bullying (recognizing, refusing, and reporting). The program helps children develop friendship skills and focuses on changing bystander behavior that supports bullying. The program teaches students and adults how to respond to bullying. According to information on their Web site, Steps to Respect is based on research demonstrating that teaching certain skills is an effective method of reducing bullying behavior. The entire school staff attends 3-hour all-staff training. This training increases adult awareness of bullying at school and teaches adults how to respond effectively to children's reports of bullying. Lessons focus on building student's skills in making and keeping friends, solving problems, managing emotions, and responding to bullying. Effective teacher interventions to reduce bullying in classrooms include empathy scaffolding, brief individual coaching sessions with students involved in bullying situations, and emotion regulation. More information about this program is available at the Committee for Children Web site at: http://www. cfchildren.org/programs/str/overview/.

in the field have led to some adaptations of the program to help ensure that it fits different cultural contexts" (Olweus & Limber, 2010, p. 126).

Bully-Proofing Your School (BPYS) was developed in 1994 as a comprehensive prevention program designed to reduce bullying at the elementary level. Based on the pioneering ideas of Olweus, a schoolwide, systemic bullying intervention with teacher training and a student curriculum was developed. The focus of BPYS is on creating a safer school environment for all by creating, nurturing, and sustaining a culture within the school that is not conducive to acts of physical, verbal, or social aggression (Porter, Plog, Jens, Garrity, Sager, & Jimerson, 2010).

Steps to Respect is a school-based program designed to decrease bullying in elementary schools and help children build more respectful, caring peer

---

relationships. Lessons in the Steps to Respect Program "promote empathic understanding of the feelings of others. The lessons aim to reduce perceptions that victims are 'outsiders' by emphasizing emotional understanding and support of peers who are excluded or harassed" (Frey et al., 2011, p. 269). Steps to Respect has "been shown to reduce the kinds of by-stander behaviors that encourage bullying" (Viadero, 2010, p. 18).

Some bullying prevention programs work well in Europe but do not work as well in the United States (Rodkin, 2011). Some of this difference can be explained by a number of challenges in adopting and implementing whole-school, comprehensive, antibullying programs with fidelity in U.S. schools. Olweus & Limber (2010) have identified and described a number of these challenges (see Box 6.3). Another challenge in adopting and implementing whole-school, comprehensive antibullying programs is the lack of adequate financial support at the state level. Research indicates that "legislative requirements for bullying prevention programs, such as whole-school bullying education, often represent unfunded mandates, leaving schools to reallocate scarce resources to fund implementation" (Institute of Education Sciences, 2011, p. 45).

Integrating Bullying Prevention Strategies Into Schoolwide Positive Behavior Support

A promising way of addressing these implementation challenges is to integrate bullying prevention strategies within existing approaches such as Schoolwide Positive Behavior Support. SWPBS is a "proactive, systems-level approach that provides the tools and practices to help support students and staff and promote positive social and learning environments" (Good, McIntosh, & Gietz, 2011, p. 50). SWPBS uses a three-tier approach that ensures the support of all students. In the primary tier, the focus is on simple preventive strategies, such as establishing, teaching, and acknowledging positively stated school expectations, and using that language regularly throughout the school day. Previous research has shown that the majority of students, sometimes as many as 80%, will respond to primary tier interventions that are implemented with integrity (Simonsen, Sugai, & Negron, 2008). Secondary and tertiary intervention strategies target those students who do not respond to primary interventions and need more targeted and intensive support (Fairbanks, Simonsen, & Sugai, 2008). Numerous studies "demonstrate the effectiveness of individualized secondary and tertiary interventions on improving students' academic and

Box 6.3 Challenges in Implementing Whole-School, Comprehensive, Evidenced-Based Bullying Prevention Programs in U.S. Schools

- Resistance on the part of staff and parents—efforts to introduce and sustain a comprehensive bullying prevention program may be doomed if a majority of school staff do not believe that bullying is a serious issue or believe that students need to deal with bullying on their own. The attitudes of the school principal about bullying prevention are particularly important to the success of a comprehensive schoolwide program.
- Desires for simple, short-term solutions to bullying. What is required to reduce bullying is nothing less than a change in the school "culture" and in the norms for behavior. This message may be hard for many to hear.
- A tendency by school personnel to "cherry pick" program elements that are perceived as easier to implement, while failing to implement those elements that pose bigger challenges.
- Zero tolerance for bullying—rather than be excluded, bullies need positive, prosocial role models.
- State laws typically require the establishment of bullying prevention policies, but few require research-based approaches to prevention and intervention. As a result, what exists in American schools is a hodgepodge of efforts to address bullying, many of which are short-term and/or "quick fixes" that are unlikely to have significant effects on the culture of bullying within schools.
- Comprehensive, research-based bullying prevention efforts require additional training, personnel, and material resources. This may a difficult "sell" in difficult economic times.

Source: Adapted from Olweus & Limber, 2010.

social behaviors" (Good, McIntosh, & Gietz, 2011, p. 51). For individuals who are interested in learning more about Schoolwide Positive Behavior Support, it can be accessed at http://www.pbis.org/.

Innovative Approaches Designed to Combat Bullying

Several programs across the United States are using shelter dogs to combat bullying. Healing Species, which began in South Carolina around 2001, addresses bullying with the assistance of rescued dogs. This program engages youth with stories, exercises, videos, and discussions of rescued animals in an effort to help students learn and practice respect for the feelings of others, and appropriate ways to respond to a bully. Students also learn how to gain power through acts of kindness and respect. Professional, trained instructors with a temperament-tested rescued dog deliver each lesson in the 13-week course. Detailed information about Healing Species can be found at: http://www.healingspecies.org/program.

The No More Bullies program, which started around 2007, in Kansas City schools, also uses canine friends to help children and youth learn empathy, respect for others, compassion, social skills, responsibility, and self-control. Ex-teacher Jo Dean Hearn, a humane education director at the animal rescue group Wayside Waifs, developed the curriculum. Hearn states that "children can easily identify with an animal and it's easy for them to transition when we ask them to consider how an animal feels (if ill treated) to how the kid sitting near them feels (if poorly treated)" (Peters, 2011, para. 3). Independent research found that the No More Bullies program resulted in a 55% decrease in suspensions, a 62% decrease in acts of aggression, and a 42% increase in acts of empathy (Peters).

Another program utilizing shelter dogs is Mutt-i-grees, which was developed at the Yale University School of the 21st Century and the Pet Savers Foundation of North Shore Animal League of America. According to information contained on its Web site, Mutt-i-grees builds on children's affinity for animals and highlights the unique characteristics and desirability of shelter dogs. The Mutt-i-grees curriculum consists of at least 25 age-appropriate 30-minute lessons and focuses on teaching social and emotional skills. In a series of easily implemented lessons, children learn critical skills that will help them in their interactions with people and animals. According to its founders, this curriculum is unique in its bridging of humane education with the emerging field of social and emotional learning (SEL). Mutt-i-grees is in 900 schools in 28 states. Detailed information about Mutt-i-grees can be found at http://education. muttigrees.org/.

The Recent Emergence of Tough Antibullying Laws Across the United States

In October 2010, the U.S. Education Department sent a clear signal to schools to take a stronger stance on bullying "with a 'Dear Colleague' letter reminding schools that failure to properly address bullying cases could violate students' civil rights" (Zubrzycki, 2011, p. 16). In their letter, the DOE (Department of Education) stated that educators need to look beyond single incidents of bullying and examine the nature of the conduct for civil rights violations. If the bullying behavior is based on perceptions about someone's race, color, national origin, sex, or disability—and if the conduct creates a hostile environment—school administrators are expected, by law, to respond with civil rights in mind (Costello, 2010a).

In reaction to the U.S. Department of Education's actions as well as public concerns about a series of high-profile suicides linked to bullying over the past several years, a growing number of states have passed antibullying legislation (Zubrzycki, 2011). As of July 2012, a total of 49 states have passed antibullying legislation and 45 states contain prohibitions against electronic harassment. Montana is the only state that currently has no such laws (Hinduja&Patchin, 2012).

According to a recent analysis of state bullying legislation, 45 state laws direct school districts to adopt bullying policies, 43 states include descriptions of bullying behavior that is prohibited under the law, 3 states prohibit bullying without defining the prohibited actions or behaviors, 36 states now include provisions in their education codes prohibiting cyberbullying or bullying using electronic media, 13 states specify that schools have jurisdiction over off-campus bullying behavior if it creates a hostile school environment, and referrals for mental health counseling are covered in only 11 state laws (Institute of Education Sciences, 2011).

Perhaps the toughest and farthest-reaching of the new state laws is New Jersey's antibullying legislation—the Anti-Bullying Bill of Rights Act (Hu, 2011). New Jersey's new law requires all public schools to adopt comprehensive antibullying policies (there are 18 pages of "required components"), increase staff training and adhere to tight deadlines for reporting episodes, and designate an antibullying specialist to investigate complaints, and the State Education Department will evaluate every effort and post grades on its Web site. Superintendents said that educators who fail to comply could lose their licenses (Hu, 2011; Zubrzycki, 2011). In addition to New Jersey, Iowa passed an antibullying law that was "hailed as one of the best in the country" when it was passed in 2007 (Wiser, 2011, p. 1). Iowa's antibullying law "requires school districts to record and report any incident of bullying, the reason for the bullying, and any action the school takes because of the incident. School administrators have four categories to choose from when they record a reason for bullying: physical attributes, race or ethnicity, real or perceived sexual orientation, and other. Districts have the latitude to carry out the policy as they see fit, as long as they record it and report it to the state" (Wiser, 2011, pp. 1–2). Because Iowa school districts, on average, reported that less than 2% of their students had been bullied in any given year since the state passed its antibullying law in 2007, the Iowa Department of Education will pilot a more comprehensive antibullying policy in select school districts before expanding it statewide during the 2012–2013 school year. Their new pilot policy has 17 categories and includes verbal, physical, and electronic bullying (Wiser, 2011).

Several trends in recent state antibullying legislation are noteworthy. These tends are: (1) expansion of the definition of bullying to include cyberbullying; (2) spelling out the potential victims of bullying, such as students who are gay, lesbian, bisexual, or transgender; (3) increasing protections for victims of bullying and those who report it; and (4) mandating professional development for teachers and education for students on the issue (Zubrzycki, 2011, p. 16). One of the most highly contentious issues is whether state antibullying laws should include provisions that specifically enumerate certain student populations (i.e., LGBT students and students with disabilities), who have been shown to be at greater risk of being victimized by bullies (American Foundation for Suicide Prevention, 2011).

Several challenges have also emerged in the development and implementation of recent state antibullying legislation. Since there is no standard definition of bullying that is universally accepted in the research field or at the federal level, the states must establish their own definitions through legislative debate and administrative action. States must define bullying by considering the specific behaviors, intent, and degree of harm to the victim (Institute of Education Sciences, 2011). A difficult legal challenge is proving the intent of the bully—a key characteristic of bullying (American Foundation for Suicide Prevention, 2011). In certain cases, the language used in legislation to define bullying has been either too broad or too specific to provide adequate protection to victims (Sacks & Salem, 2009). In addition, the way that bullying is defined in law has important implications for how behavior is viewed within the school community and the extent to which school personnel and other students recognize and respond to bullying situations (Swearer, Limber, & Alley, 2009). A significant challenge in defining bullying is determining when developmentally appropriate problem behavior, such as teasing, progresses into more serious misconduct that warrants intervention or disciplinary action. The growth of cyberbullying "introduces added challenges to defining conduct that reasonably requires school action or enforcement" (Institute of Education Sciences, 2011, p. 25).

A very thorough, detailed analysis of current state bullying laws and policies published by the U.S. Department of Education is available on the Department's Web site at http://www.ed.gov/about/offices/list/opepd/ppss/index.html. Recent state antibullying legislation can also be tracked at the Bully Police USA Web site (http://www.bullypolice.org/). This Web site was founded by Brenda High, whose son hanged himself by his backpack strap just after his 12th birthday. It provides grades to each state according to the comprehensiveness and effectiveness of its antibullying legislation (Franks, 2010).

In the End—Combating Bullying Is a Human Rights Issue

Perhaps one of the most powerful vantage points for raising consciousness and rallying the support of others to combat bullying is by viewing bullying within a human rights framework (Levesque, 2001). Greene (2006) provides a compelling case for adopting and infusing a human rights perspective as a means of increasing the effectiveness and sustainability of school-based bullying prevention programs by stating that "[a] human rights perspective is predicated on the assumption that all human beings are entitled to an inalienable set of rights 'simply because of their human status' and that organizations such as schools have an obligation to uphold human rights standards ... [which includes the] right for a child to feel safe in school and to be spared the oppression and repeated, intentional humiliation" (Greene, 2006, pp. 73–74). A human rights perspective also forces us to broaden the scope of antibullying efforts to include those actions and circumstances that create "hostile environments." For example, students should not have to attend schools where bullying incidents among students are routinely ignored by adults or where sexual jokes and innuendos are condoned or where bullying exists among teachers and administrators (Galloway & Roland, 2004). A human rights perspective can also serve to encourage victimized students and witnesses to intervene and report instances of bullying or human rights violations to authorities and overcome a "culture of silence" (Greene, 2006, p. 73).

Summary

Bullying does not lend itself to the same interventions that may be effective in addressing other types of peer conflict. Bullying can be reduced substantially by implementing a comprehensive, whole-school approach that modifies all levels of the social ecology of the school (i.e., school-level, classroom-level, and student-level). A number of best-practice strategies at each of these levels have been developed. Several empirically supported bullying prevention programs based on a whole-school, comprehensive approach have also been implemented including, the Olweus Bullying Prevention Program, Bully-Proofing Your School, and Steps to Respect.

There are a number of challenges in adopting and implementing whole-school, comprehensive antibullying programs with fidelity in U.S. schools. One promising way of addressing these implementation challenges is to integrate bullying prevention strategies within existing approaches such as Schoolwide Positive Behavior Support. Several programs across the U.S. (Healing Species, No More Bullies, and Mutt-i-grees) are also using shelter dogs to combat bullying. Over the past several years, a total of 47 states have passed antibullying legislation. Only Michigan, Montana, and South Dakota have no such laws, and all but six state laws contain prohibitions against cyberbullying. Perhaps the toughest and farthest-reaching of the new state laws is New Jersey's antibullying legislation. In addition to New Jersey, Iowa passed an antibullying law that was "hailed as one of the best in the country" when it was passed in 2007. One of the most highly contentious issues is whether state antibullying laws should include provisions that specifically enumerate certain student populations (i.e., LGBT students and students with disabilities), who have been shown to be at greater risk of being victimized by bullies. A difficult legal challenge facing each state in defining bullying in its state laws is proving the intent of the bully—a key characteristic of bullying.

Perhaps one of the most powerful vantage points for raising consciousness and rallying the support of others to combat bullying is by viewing bullying within a human rights framework, namely, that all human beings are entitled to an inalienable set of rights "simply because of their human status" and that organizations such as schools have an obligation to uphold human rights standards, which include the right for a child to feel safe in school and to be spared the oppression and repeated, intentional humiliation.

Appendix

Bullying Assessment Tools

Hamburger, M. E., Basile, K. C., & Vivolo, A. M. (2011). *Measuring bullying victimization, perpetration, and bystander experiences: A compendium of assessment tools.* Atlanta, GA: Centers for Disease Control and Prevention, National Center for Injury Prevention and Control.

This compendium provides researchers, prevention specialists, and health educators with tools to measure a range of bullying experiences: bully perpetration, bully victimization, bully-victim experiences, and bystander experiences. This compendium represents a starting point from which researchers can consider a set of psychometrically sound measures for assessing self-reported incidence and prevalence of a variety of bullying experiences. This compendium includes measures of bully perpetration only (Section A: Bully Only); bully victimization only (Section B: Victim Only); being both a bully and a victim (Section C: Bully and Victim); and being a bully, a bystander (observer), and/or a victim of bullying situations (Section D: Bystander, Bully, and/or Victim).

Bullying Prevention Curricula and Fact Sheets

StopBullying.gov

StopBullying.gov provides information from various government agencies on how kids, teens, young adults, parents, educators, and others in the community can prevent or stop bullying. All of these resource kits can be downloaded from www.stopbullying.gov.

Anti-Defamation League

The ADL is a leader in developing antibullying and anti-cyberbullying training, curriculum, and resources for teens, school educators, youth providers, and adult family members. ADL provides the tools and resources to assist people in taking action to prevent and respond to bullying and cyberbullying. See http://www.adl.org/combatbullying/.

The ADL has also developed a model Cyberbullying Prevention Law for states to adopt and implement. The policy gives schools the resources they need to combat and respond to bully ing and cyberbullying. This model statute can be found at http://www.adl.org/main_internet/Cyberbullying_Prevention_Law.

Special Issue of Excellence and Ethics

A special issue of *Excellence and Ethics* focuses on bullying, promoting kindness, and creating a safe and supportive learning environment. See http://www2.cortland.edu/dotAsset/a7bc96d9-acad-472c-8ae4-a1891781a0d6.pdf.

Connect for Respect

In March 2011, National PTA® launched an initiative to encourage PTAs across the country to lead conversations in their school communities about bullying and how it is affecting their communities, and to develop solutions that they can implement collaboratively together. This Web site contains tools and resources that PTAs can use to plan their **Connect for Respect** events. See http://www.pta.org/bullying.asp.

Cyberbullying Resources

Seattle Public Schools—Middle School Cyberbullying Curriculum

This curriculum educates teachers about cyberbullying and includes a language they can share with their students. It addresses the issue of a student being a bystander to being a victim to being a bully at different times and how to resist the urge to "bully back." The curriculum focuses on writing and asks students to write personal contracts about their online behavior. It also involves parents by utilizing take-home letters and activities. See http://district.seattleschools.org/modules/cms/pages.phtml?pageid=216981.

Cyberbullying Research Center

The Cyberbullying Research Center is dedicated to providing up-to-date information about the nature, extent, causes, and consequences of cyberbullying among adolescents. This Web site serves as a clearinghouse of information concerning the ways adolescents use and misuse technology. It is intended to be a resource for parents, educators, law enforcement officers, counselors, and others who work with youth. Here you will find facts, figures, and detailed stories from those who have been directly impacted by online aggression. In addition, the site includes numerous resources to help you prevent and respond to cyberbullying incidents. The Cyberbullying Research Center is directed by Dr. Sameer Hinduja (Florida Atlantic University) and Dr. Justin Patchin (University of Wisconsin-Eau Claire). They have been studying cyberbullying since 2002 and first launched this Web site in 2005. They founded the Center as a means to further their mission of bringing sound research about cyberbullying to those who can benefit most from it. See http://www.cyberbullying.us/.

WiredSafety.org

WiredSafety.org is a U.S. charity operating through its volunteers worldwide. It is the largest and oldest online safety, education, and help group in the world. Originating in 1995 as a group of volunteers rating Web sites, it now provides one-to-one help, extensive information, and education to cyberspace users of all ages on a myriad of Internet and interactive technology safety, privacy, and security issues. These services are offered through a worldwide organization comprised entirely of unpaid volunteers who administer specialized Web sites, resources, and programs. See http://www.wiredsafety.org/.

Embracing Digital Youth

Embracing Digital Youth (a program of Center for Safe and Responsible Internet Use) promotes approaches that will best ensure all young people become "cybersavvy" and address youth risk in a positive and restorative manner. See http://www.embracingdigitalyouth.org/.

Netcetera

The Net Cetera Community Outreach Toolkit helps you provide the people in your community with information about protecting kids online. Regardless of your experience as a speaker—or your expertise in online safety—this kit has the resources and information you need to convey key points about protecting kids online. See http://www.onguardonline.gov/topics/net-cetera. aspx.

GLBTQ Bullying Resources

Gay, Lesbian and Straight Education Network
GLSEN, or the **Gay, Lesbian and Straight Education Network**, is the leading national education organization focused on ensuring safe schools for all students. GLSEN envisions a world in which every child learns to respect and

accept all people, regardless of sexual orientation or gender identity/expression. For more information on GLSEN's research, educational resources, public policy agenda, student organizing programs, or development initiatives, visit www.glsen.org.

Parents, Families and Friends of Lesbians and Gays (PFLAG)

Parents, Families and Friends of Lesbians and Gays (PFLAG) is a national nonprofit organization with over 200,000 members and supporters and over 350 affiliates in the United States. This vast grassroots network is cultivated, resourced, and serviced by the PFLAG National Office, located in Washington, D.C., the national Board of Directors, and 13 Regional Directors. See http://community.pflag.org/page.aspx?pid=191.

It Gets Better Project

The It Gets Better Project was created to show young LGBT people the levels of happiness, potential, and positivity their lives will reach—if they can just get through their teen years. The It Gets Better Project wants to remind teenagers in the LGBT community that they are not alone—and it *will* get better. See http://www.itgetsbetter.org/.

Planned Parenthood

Planned Parenthood provides high-quality, sensitive, and appropriate reproductive health, general health, and sexual health services to all lesbian, gay, bisexual, and transgender (LGBT) patients. See http://www.plannedparenthood.org/health-topics/sexual-orientation-gender-4329.htm.

American Academy of Pediatrics

The American Academy of Pediatrics issued its first statement on homosexuality and adolescents in 1983, with a revision in 1993. This 2004 report reflects the growing understanding of youth of differing sexual orientations. It contains definitions of sexual orientation, gender identity, gender role, transgendered individuals, and transvestites. It also includes sections on etiology and prevalence, special needs of nonheterosexual and questioning youth, comprehensive health care for all adolescents, and community advocacy. See http://aappolicy.aappublications.org/cgi/content/full/pediatrics;113/6/1827.

Project 10

The Project 10 Web site includes links to a bill of rights for gay and lesbian students, how to deal with the opposition, and a teacher's self-evaluation of nonbiased behavior. See www.project10.org.

It's Elementary. Talking About Gay Issues

This 78-minute documentary makes a case that children should be taught to respect all people, including lesbians and gay men, as part of their early education. It is designed to inspire teachers and administrators to take the next steps at their own schools to increase student knowledge and sensitivity for this aspect of diversity. This videotape may be obtained through Women's Educational Media, 2180 Bryant St., Suite 203, San Francisco, CA 94110. Telephone: (415) 641-4616. E-mail: wemfilms@womedia.org.

Sexual Bullying/Sexual Harassment

Smith, J., Huppuch, M., & Van Deven, M. (and Girls for Gender Equity). (2011). *Hey, shorty!: A guide to combating sexual harassment and violence in schools and on the streets.* New York: The Feminist Press at CUNY.

References

Allen, K. P. (2010). A bullying intervention system: Reducing risk and creating support for aggressive students. *Preventing School Failure, 54*, 199–209.

American Civil Liberties Union. (n.d.). *The ACLU and freedom of religion and belief.* Retrieved from http://www.aclu.org/religion-belief/aclu-and-freedom-religion-and-belief

American Foundation for Suicide Prevention. (2011, July 18). *State anti-bullying laws.* Washington, DC: Author.

American Psychological Association. (2011). *Sexual orientation and homosexuality.* Retrieved from http://www.apa.org/helpcenter/sexual-orientation.aspx

Ang, R. P., & Goh, D. H. (2010). Cyberbullying among adolescents: The role of affective and cognitive empathy, and gender. *Child Psychiatry and Human Development, 41*, 387–397.

Apter, S. J., & Propper, C. A. (1986). Ecological perspectives on youth violence. In S. J. Apter & A. P. Goldstein (Eds.), *Youth violence: Programs and prospects* (pp. 140–159). Oxford, UK: Pergamon Press.

Banyard, V. L., Cross, C., & Modecki, K. L. (2006). Interpersonal violence in adolescence: Ecological correlates of self-reported perpetration. *Journal of Interpersonal Violence, 21*, 1314–1332.

Barboza, G. E., Schiamberg, L. B., Oehmke, J., Korzeniewski, S. J., Post, L. A., & Heraux, C.G. (2009). Individual characteristics and the multiple contexts of adolescent bullying: An ecological perspective. *Journal of Youth and Adolescence, 38*, 101–121.

Bartkowski, J. (1996). Beyond biblical literalism and inerrancy: Conservative Protestants and the hermeneutic interpretation of scripture. *Sociology of Religion, 57*, 259–272.

Belenardo, S. J. (2001). Practices and conditions that lead to a sense of community in middle schools. *NASSP Bulletin, 85*, 1–7.

Benson, J. (2011, July 11). Psychiatrist says video games are influencing youth, and not for the better. *The Day.* Retrieved from http://www.theday.com/article/20110602/NWS01/306029399

Beran, T., & Li, Q. (2007). The relationship between cyberbullying and school bullying. *Journal of Student Wellbeing, 1*(2), 15–33.

Blosnich, J., & Bossarte, R. (2011). Low-level violence in schools: Is there an association between school safety measures and peer victimization? *Journal of School Health, 81*, 107–113.

Blumenfeld, W. J. (2006). Christian privilege and the promotion of "secular" and not-so "secular" mainline Christianity in public schooling and in the larger society. *Equity & Excellence in Education, 39*, 195–210.

Borg, M. (1999). The extent and nature of bullying among primary and secondary school- children. *British Journal of Educational Psychology, 62,* 137–153.

Boulton, M., & Underwood, K. (1992). Bully/victim problems among middle school children. *Developmental Psychology, 25,* 320–330.

Boxer, P., Edwards-Leeper, L., Goldstein, S. E., Musher-Eizenman, D., & Dubow, E. F. (2003). Exposure to "low-level" aggression in school: Associations with aggressive behavior, future expectations, and perceived safety. *Violence and Victims, 18,* 691–705.

Boyd, D., & Marwick, A. (2011, September 23). Bullying as true drama. *The New York Times,* A35.

Brody, J. E. (2010, February 16). Empathy's natural, but nurturing it helps. *The New York Times,* D7.

Cass, C., & Anderson, S. A. (2011, September 27). Poll: Young people say online meanness pervasive. *The Huffington Post.* Retrieved from http://www.huffingtonpost.com/2011/09/27/poll-young-people-say-onl_n_982834.html

Centers for Disease Control and Prevention. (2011). Bullying among middle school and high school students—Massachusetts, 2009. *MMWR, 60,* 465–496.

Center for Mental Health in Schools at UCLA. (2011). *Embedding bullying interventions into a comprehensive system of student and learning supports. A Center policy & practice brief.* Los Angeles: Author.

Center for School Mental Health Assistance. (2002). *Bullying resource packet.* Baltimore: University of Maryland.

Child Welfare Information Gateway. (2011). *Definitions of child abuse and neglect.* Washington, DC: U.S. Department of Health and Human Services, Children's Bureau.

Christenson, P., & Ivancin, M. (2006). *The "reality" of health: Reality television and the public health.* Menlo Park, CA: The Henry J. Kaiser Family Foundation.

Cohn, A., & Canter, A. (2003). Bullying: Facts for schools and parents. Retrieved from National Association of School Psychologists Web site: http://www.naspcenter.org

Coivin, G., Tobin, T., Beard, K., Hadan, S., & Sprague, J. (1998). The school bully: Assessing the problem, developing interventions, and future research direction. *Journal of Behavioral Education, 8,* 293–319.

Cole, A. H., Jr. (2006). Working with families from religious fundamentalist backgrounds. In C. Franklin, M. B. Harris, & P. Allen-Meares (Eds.), *School services sourcebook: A guide for school-based professionals* (471–499). New York: Oxford University Press.

Costello, M. (2010a). Bullying is a civil rights issue. *Teaching tolerance.* Montgomery, AL: Southern Poverty Law Center.

Costello, M. (2010b). Focus on the Family goes after LGBT students. Southern Poverty Law Center. Retrieved from Teaching tolerance Web site: www.tolerance.org

Craig, W. M. (1998). The relationship among bullying, victimization, depression, anxiety, and aggression in elementary school children. *Personal and Individual Differences, 24,* 123–130.

Craig, W. M., Pepler, D., & Atlas, R. (2000). Observations of bullying in the playground and in the classroom. *School Psychology International, 21,* 22–36.

Crick, N. R., Nelson, D. A., Morales, J. R., Cullerton-Sen, C., Casas, J. F., & Hickman, S.E. (2001). Relational victimization in childhood and adolescence: I hurt you through the grapevine. In J. Juvonen and S. Graham (Eds.), *Peer harassment in school: The plight of the vulnerable and victimized* (pp. 196–214). New York: Guilford Press.

Croucher, R. (and others). (2009). *Religious bullying.* Retrieved from http://jmm.aaa.net.au/articles/22258.htm

Cunningham, P. B., Henggeler, S. W., Limber, S. P., Melton, G. B., and Nation, M. A. (2000). Patterns and correlates of gun ownership among nonmetropolitan and rural middle school students. *Journal of Clinical Child Psychology, 29,* 432–442.

Cushman, C. (2010). *The problem with politicized bullying policies.* Cititzen Link. Retrieved from http://www.citizenlink.com/2010/06/14/the-problem-with-politicized-bullying-policies/

Darling, N. (2010). Teasing and bullying, boys and girls. Retrieved from www.psychologytoday.com/print/49693

D'Augelli, A., Grossman, A., Salter, N., Vasey, J., Starks, M., & Sinclair, K. (2005). Predicting the suicide attempts of lesbian, gay, and bisexual youth. *Suicide & Life-Threatening Behavior, 35,* 646–660.

David-Ferdon C., & Hertz M. F. (2009). *Electronic media and youth violence: A CDC issue brief for researchers.* Atlanta, GA: Centers for Disease Control.

Dawkins, J. L. (1996). Bullying, physical disability and the pediatric patient. *Developmental Medicine and Child Neurology, 38,* 603–612.

DeHue, F., Bolman, C., & Völlink, T. (2008). Cyberbullying: Youngsters' experiences and parental perception. *CyberPsychology & Behavior, 11,* 217–223.

Delmonico, D. L., & Griffin, E. J. (2008). Cybersex and the e-teen: What marriage and family therapists should know. *Journal of Marital and Family Therapy, 34,* 431–444.

Devine, J. F. (1996). *Maximum security: The culture of violence in inner-city schools.* Chicago: University of Chicago Press.

DeVoe, J. F., Kaffenberger, S., and Chandler, K. (2005). Student reports of bullying results: From the 2001 school crime supplement to the National Crime Victimization Survey. Retrieved from National Center for Education Statistics Web site: http://nces.ed.gov/pubs2005/2005310.pdf

Diaz, E. M., Kosciw, J. G., & Greytak, E.A. (2010). School connectedness for lesbian, gay, bisexual, and transgender youth: In-school victimization and institutional supports. *The Prevention Researcher, 17,* 15–17.

Doll, B., Song, S., Champion, A., & Jones, K. (2011). Classroom ecologies that support or discourage bullying. In D. L. Espelage & S. M. Swearer (Eds.), *Bullying in North American Schools* (2nd ed., pp. 147–158). New York: Routledge.

Draper, E. (2010, August 29). Focus on Family says anti-bullying efforts in schools push gay agenda. *The Denver Post.* Retrieved from http://www.denverpost.com/news/ci_15928224?IADID=Search-www.denverpost.com-www.denverpost.com

Duncan, R. D. (2011). Family relationships of bullies and victims. In D. L. Espelage & S. M. Swearer (Eds.), *Bullying in North American Schools* (2nd ed., pp. 191–204). New York: Routledge.

Dupper, D. R. (2010). *A new model of school discipline: Engaging students and preventing behavior problems.* New York: Oxford University Press.

Dupper, D. R., & Meyer-Adams, N. (2002). Low-level violence: A neglected aspect of school culture. *Urban Education, 37,* 350–364.

Durlak, J. A., Taylor, R. D., Kawashima, K., Pachan, M. K., DuPre, E. R., Celio, C. I., et al. (2007). Effects of positive youth development programs on school, family, and community systems. *American Journal of Community Psychology, 39*, 269–286.

Eckholm, E. (2011a, December 28). Battling anew over the place of religion in public schools. *New York Times*, A10.

Eckholm, E. (2011b, September 13). In suburb, battle goes public on bullying of gay students. *New York Times*, A1.

Eliot, M., Cornell, D., Gregory, A., & Fan, X. (2010). Supportive school climate and student willingness to seek help for bullying and threats of violence. *Journal of School Psychology, 48*, 533–553.

Espelage, D. L. (2004). An ecological perspective to school-based bullying prevention. *The Prevention Researcher, 11*, 3–6.

Espelage, D., Stein, N., Rose, C., & Elliot, J. (2009, April). *Middle school bullying & sexual violence: Unique & shared predictors*. Paper presented at the American Educational Research Association Conference, San Diego, CA.

Fagan, A. A., Hawkins, J. D., & Catalano, R. F. (2008). Using community epidemiologic data to improve social settings: The Communities That Care prevention system. In M. Shin (Ed.), *Toward positive youth development: Transforming schools and community programs* (pp. 292–312). Oxford, UK; New York: Oxford University Press.

Fairbanks, S., Simonsen, B., & Sugai, G. (2008). Classwide secondary and tertiary tier practices and systems. *Teaching Exceptional Children, 40*, 44–52.

Faris, R., & Felmlee, D. (2011). Status struggles: Network centrality and gender segregation in same- and cross-gender aggression. *American Sociological Review, 76*, 48–73.

Farmer, T. W., Petrin, R. A., Robertson, D. L., Fraser, M. W., Hall, C. M., Day, S. H., et al. (2010). Peer relations of bullies, bully-victims, and victims: The two social worlds of bullying in second-grade classrooms. *Elementary School Journal, 110*, 364–392.

Farrington, D. (1993). Understanding and preventing bullying. In M. Tonry (Ed.), *Crime and Justice: A review of research* (Vol. 17, pp. 381–458). Chicago: University of Chicago Press.

Farrington, D. P., & Ttofi, M. M. (2010). *School-based programs to reduce bullying and victimization*. Report submitted to the U.S. Department of Justice. Retrieved from http://www.ncjrs.gov/pdffiles1/nij/grants/229377.pdf

Fox, J. A., Elliot, D. S., Kerlikowske, R. G., Newman, S. A., & Christenson, W. (2003). *Bullying prevention is crime prevention*. Washington, DC: Fight Crime: Invest in Kids. Retrieved from http://www.fightcrime.org/state/usa/reports/bullying-prevention-crime-prevention-2003

Franks, L. (2010, March 31). How to stop a bully. *The Daily Beast*. Retrieved from http://www.thedailybeast.com/articles/2010/03/31/how-to-stop-a-bully.html

Freiberg, H. J., & Lapointe, J. M. (2006). Research-based programs for preventing and solving discipline problems. In C. M. Evertson & C. S. Weinstein (Eds.), *Handbook of classroom management: Research, practice, and contemporary issues* (pp. 735–786). Mahwah, NJ: Erlbaum.

Freiberg, H. J., & Stein, T. A. (1999). Measuring, improving and sustaining healthy learning environments. In H. J. Freiberg (Ed.), *School climate: Measuring, improving and sustaining healthy learning environments*. London: Falmer Press.

Frey, K. S., Edstrom, L. V., & Hirschstein, M. K. (2010). School bullying: A crisis or an opportunity? In S. R. Jimerson, S. M. Swearer, & D. L. Espelage (Eds.), *Handbook of bullying in schools: An international perspective* (pp. 403–415). New York: Routledge.

Frey, K. S., Carlson Jones, D., Hirschstein, M. K., & Edstrom, L. V. (2011). Teacher support of bullying prevention: The good, the bad, and the promising. In D. L. Espelage & S. M. Swearer (Eds.), *Bullying in North American schools* (2nd ed., pp. 266–277). New York: Routledge.

Furlong, M. J., Chung, A., Bates, M., & Morrison, R. L. (1995). Who are the victims of school violence? A comparison of student non-victims and multi-victims. *Education and Treatment of Children, 18,* 282–298.

Galloway, D., & Roland, E. (2004). Is the direct approach to reducing bullying always the best? In P. K. Smith, D. Pepler, & K. Rigby (Eds.), *Bullying in schools: How successful can interventions be?* (pp. 37–53). Cambridge, UK: Cambridge University Press.

Garbarino, J., & deLara, E. (2003). Words can hurt forever. *Educational Leadership, 60*(6), 18–21.

Gastic, B. (2008). School truancy and the disciplinary problems of bullying victims. *Educational Review, 60*(4), 391–404.

Gay, Lesbian and Straight Education Network (GLSEN). (n.d.). *Institutional heterosexism in our schools: A guide to understanding and undoing it.* New York: GLSEN. Retrieved on October 9, 2011 from www.glsen.org

Gay, Lesbian and Straight Education Network (GLSEN). (2010). *The 2009 national climate survey: Executive summary.* New York: Author.

Gini, G. (2008). Associations between bullying behavior, psychosomatic complaints, emotional, and behavioral problems. *Journal of Pediatrics and Child Health, 44,* 492–497.

Goldstein, A. P. (1999). *Low-level aggression.* Champaign, IL: Research Press.

Good, C. P., McIntosh, K., & Gietz, C. (2011, Sept./Oct.). Integrating bullying prevention into school-wide positive behavior support. *Teaching Exceptional Children, 44,* 48–56.

Goodemann, C., Zammitt, K. A., & Hagedorn, M. (in press). The wolf in sheep's clothing: Student harassment veiled as bullying. *Children & Schools.*

Goodwin, B. (2011). Bullying is common—And subtle. *Educational Leadership, 69,* 82–83.

Gore-Oleksiw, K. A. (2011). Bullying – no longer just in schools, West Hartford's proactive approach. Retrieved on October 30, 2011 from http://www.westhartfordnews.com/articles/2011/06/16/news/doc4df92a57051e4166359924.txt

Gould, J. E. (2011, August 5). Seth's law: Can a bullied boy leave California a legal legacy? *Time Magazine.* Retrieved from http://www.time.com/time/nation/article/0,8599,2086521,00.html

Graham, S. (2009). Some myths and facts about bullies and victims. In S. Hymel & S. M. Swearer (Eds.), *Bullying at school and online* (special edition of *Education.com*). Retrieved from http://www.education.com/reference/article/bullying-myths-facts/?page=3

Greene, M. B. (2006). Bullying in schools: A plea for measure of human rights. *Journal of Social Issues, 62*, 63–79.

Gruber, J. E., & Fineran, S. (2008). Comparing the impact of bullying and sexual harassment victimization on the mental and physical health of adolescents. *Sex Roles, 59*, 1–13.

Guerra, N. G., Williams, K. R., & Sadek, S. (2011). Understanding bullying and victimization during childhood and adolescence: A mixed methods study. *Child Development, 82*, 295–310.

Hamburger, M. E., Basile, K. C., & Vivolo, A. M. (2011). *Measuring bullying victimization, perpetration, and bystander experiences: A compendium of assessment tools*. Atlanta, GA: Centers for Disease Control and Prevention, National Center for Injury Prevention and Control.

Hamilton, M. L., & Richardson, V. (1995). Effects of the culture in two schools on the process and outcomes of staff development. *Elementary School Journal, 95*, 367–385.

Harris Interactive and GLSEN. (2005). *From teasing to torment: School climate in America. A survey of students and teachers*. New York: GLSEN.

Hart, E. L., & Parmeter, S. H. (1992). Writing in the margins: A lesbian and gay inclusive course. In C. M. Hurlbert & S. Totten (Eds.), *Social issues in the English classroom* (pp. 154–173). Urbana, IL: National Council of Teachers of English. (ERIC Document Reproduction Service No. ED349574.)

Hawkins, J. D., & Catalano, R. F. (1992). *Communities that care: Action for drug abuse prevention*. San Francisco: Jossey-Bass, Inc.

Haynie, D. L., Nansel, T., Eitel P., Davis-Crump, A., Saylor, K., Yu, K., et al. (2001). Bullies, victims, and bully/victims: Distinct groups of at-risk youth. *Journal of Early Adolescence, 21*, 29–49.

Hazler, R. J. (1994). Bullying breeds violence: You can stop it. *Learning, 22*, 38–41.

Higgins, J. (2011, November 12). *Jewish family sues Green schools over bullying of girl*. Retrieved from http://www.ohio.com/news/local/jewish-family-sues-green-schools-over-bullying-of-girl-1.245047

Hill, C., & Kearl, H. (2011). *Crossing the line: Sexual harassment at school*. Washington, DC: American Association of University Women.

Hinduja, S., & Patchin, J. W. (2007). Offline consequences of online victimization: School violence and delinquency. *Journal of School Violence, 6*, 89–112.

Hinduja, S., & Patchin, J. W. (2009). *Bullying beyond the school yard: Preventing and responding to cyberbullying*. Thousand Oaks, CA: Sage Publications.

Hinduja, S., & Patchin, J. W. (2010). Bullying, cyberbullying, and suicide. *Archives of Suicide Research, 14*, 206–221.

Hinduja, S., & Patchin, J. (2011). Cyberbullying: A review of the legal issues facing educators. *Preventing School Failure, 55*, 71–78.

Hinduja, S. & Patchin, J.W. (2012). State Cyberbullying Laws: A brief review of state cyberbullying laws and policies, accessed September 18, 2012, http://www.cyberbullying.us/Bullying_and_Cyberbullying_Laws.pdf

Hoffman, J. (2010, June 28). Online bullies pull schools into fray. *The New York Times*. A1.

Holladay, J. (2010, Fall). Cyberbullying: The stakes have never been higher for students—or schools. *Teaching Tolerance, 38*, 43–46.

Holt, M., Keyes, M., & Koening, B. (2011). Teachers' attitudes toward bullying. In D. L. Espelage & S. M. Swearer (Eds.), *Bullying in North American schools* (2nd ed., pp. 119–131). New York: Routledge.

Hsiao-chuan, H. (2011, January 1). School bullying just reflects society. *Taipei Times*. Retrieved from http://220.228.147.132/News/editorials/archives/2011/01/01/2003492367

Hu, W. (2011, August 31). Bullying law puts New Jersey schools on spot. *The New York Times*, A1.

Hulsether, M. (2007). *Religion, culture and politics in the twentieth century United States*. New York: Columbia University Press.

Hyman, I. A. (1990). *Reading, writing and the hickory stick: The appalling story of physical and psychological abuse of American school children*. Lexington, MA: Lexington Books.

Hyman, I., & Perone, D. (1998). The other side of school violence: Educator policies and practices that may contribute to school misbehavior. *Journal of School Psychology*, 36, 7–27.

Hyman, I. A., & Snook, P. (2002). *My Worst School Experience Scale (MWSE)*. Los Angeles: Western Psychological Services.

Hyman, I. A., Weiler, E., Probone, D., Romano, L., Britton, G., & Shancok, A. (1997). Victims and victimizers: The two faces of school maltreatment. In A. Goldstein & J. Conoley (Eds.), *School maltreatment intervention: A practical handbook* (pp. 426–459). New York: Guilford.

Hyman, I. A., Zelikoff, W., & Clarke, J. (1988). Psychological and physical abuse in the schools: A paradigm for understanding post-traumatic stress disorder in children and youth. *Journal of Traumatic Stress*, 1, 243–267.

Hymel, S., Rocke-Henderson, N., & Bonanno, R. A. (2005). Moral disengagement: A framework for understanding bullying among adolescents [Special international issue on victimization]. *Journal of Social Sciences*, 8, 1–11.

India Tracy Campaign. (2005). *Earthward*. Retrieved from http://www.earthward.org/india.shtml

Institute of Education Sciences. (2011). *Student reports of bullying and cyber-bullying: Results from the 2009 School Crime Supplement to the National Crime Victimization Survey*. Washington, DC: U.S. Department of Education, National Center for Education Statistics.

Interfaith Report. (2008, November). *Beatbullying*. UK: Author. Retrieved from http://www.beatbullying.org/index.html

Irvine, M., & Tanner, R. (2007, October). Sex abuse a shadow over U.S. schools. *Education Week*, 27(9), pp. 1, 16–19.

Ivarsson, T., Broberg, A. G., Arvidsson, T., & Gillberg. C. (2005). Bullying in adolescence: Psychiatric problems in victims and bullies as measured by the Youth Self Report (YRS) and the Depression Self-Rating Scale (DSRS). *Nordic Journal of Psychiatry*, 59, 365–373.

Jacobson, R. B. (2010). On bullshit and bullying: Taking seriously those we educate. *Journal of Moral Education*, 39, 437–448.

Janssen, K. (2010, July 29). Chicago Public Schools crackdown on cyberbullies. *Chicago Sun Times*. Retrieved from http://suntimes.com/news/education/2546114,CST-NWS-bully29.article

Janssen, I., Craig, W. M., Boyce, W. F., & Pickett, W. (2004). Associations between overweight and obesity with bullying behaviors in school-aged children. *Pediatrics, 113,* 1187–1194.

Jenson, J. M. (2006). Advances and challenges in preventing childhood and adolescent problem behavior. *Social Work Research, 30,* 131–134.

Josephson Institute. (2010). *Largest study ever shows half of all high school students were bullies and nearly half were the victims of bullying during the past year.* Retrieved on April 10, 2011 from http://charactercounts.org/programs/reportcard/2010/installment01_report-card_bullying-youth-violence.html

Juvonen, J., & Graham, S. (2004). Research-based interventions on bullying. In C. E. Sanders & G. D. Phye (Eds.), *Bullying: Implications for the classroom* (pp. 229–255). London: Elsevier Academic Press.

Kallestad, J. H., & Olweus, D. (2003, October 1). Predicting teachers' and school's implementation of the Olweus Bullying Prevention Program: A multilevel study. *Prevention & Treatment, 6,* Article 21. Retrieved from http://journals.apa.org/prevention

Kaltiala-Heino, R., Rimpela, M., Rantanen, P., & Rimpela. A. (2000). Bullying at school—An indicator of adolescents at risk for mental disorders. *Journal of Adolescence, 23,* 661–674.

Kaufman, G. (2011, September 27). Cyberbullying, sexting widespread, MTV/AP survey reveals. Retrieved from http://www.mtv.com/news/articles/1671547/cyberbullying-sexting-mtv-ap-survey.jhtml

Kazdin, A., & Rotella, C. (2009, August 11). Bullies: They can be stopped, but it takes a village. *Slate.* Retrieved from www.slate.com/id/2249424

Kerbs, J. J., & Jolley, J. M. (2007). The joy of violence: What about violence is fun in middle school? *American Journal of Criminal Justice, 32,* 12–29.

Klomek, A. B., Marracco, F., Kleinman, M., Schonfeld, I. S., & Gould, M. S. (2007). Bullying, depression, and suicidality in adolescents. *Journal of the American Academy of Child and Adolescent Psychiatry, 46,* 40–49.

Knox, E., & Conti-Ramsden, G. (2003). Bullying risks of 11-year-old children with specific language impairment: Does school placement matter? *International Journal of Language and Communication Disorders, 38,* 1–12.

Koenig, D., & Daniels, R. H. (2011). Bully at the blackboard. *Teaching Tolerance, 40*(Fall), 58–61.

Kosciw, J. G., Diaz, E. M., & Greytak, E. A. (2008). *2007 National school climate survey: The experiences of lesbian, gay, bisexual and transgender youth in our nation's schools.* New York: GLSEN.

Kowalski, R. M., & Limber, S. P. (2007). Electronic bullying among middle school students. *Journal of Adolescent Health, 41,* S22–S30.

Levesque, R. J. R. (2001). *Culture and family violence: Fostering change through human rights law* (Law and public policy, Vol. 4). Washington, DC: American Psychological Association.

Limber, S. P. (2002, May). *Addressing youth bullying behaviors.* Proceedings from the American Medical Association Educational Forum on Adolescent Health: Youth Bullying. Chicago, IL: American Medical Association. Retrieved from www.ama-assn.org/ama1/pub/upload/mm/39/youthbullying.pdf

Limber, S. P., & Nation, M. M. (1998). Bullying among children and youth. In J. L. Arnette & M. C. Walsleben (Eds.), *Combating fear and restoring safety in schools* [Bulletin] (pp. 4–5). Washington, DC: U.S. Department of Justice, Office of Juvenile Justice and Delinquency Prevention.

Linsley, J. (2001). Working with gay and lesbian youth. *New Social Worker, 8*, 8–11.

Low, S. M., Smith, B. H., Brown, E. C., Fernandez, K., Hanson, K., & Haggerty, K. P. (2011). Design and analysis of a randomized controlled trial of Steps to Respect: A school-based bullying prevention program. In D. L. Espelage & S. M. Swearer (Eds.), *Bullying in North American schools* (2nd ed., pp. 278–290). New York: Routledge.

Lumeng, J.C., Forrest, P., Appugliese, D.P. Kaciroti, N., Corwyn, R.F. &Bradley, R.H. (2010).Weight Status as a Predictor of Being Bullied in Third Through Sixth Grades. *Pediatrics*, e1301. Retrieved from: http://pediatrics.aappublications.org/content/125/6/e1301.full.html

Macgillivray, I. K. (2004). *Sexual orientation and school policy: A practical guide for teachers, administrators, and community activists.* Lanham, MD: Rowman & Littlefield Publishers.

Marcus, K. L. (2011, May 27). IJCR blasts religious bullying. *Institute for Jewish and Community Research.* Retrieved from http://www.jewishresearch.org/v2/2011/press-releases/05-05-2011.html

Martin, C. E. (2008, July 10). Counter cyberbullies with compassion. *Christian Science Monitor.* Retrieved from http://www.csmonitor.com/layout/set/print/content/view/print/230982

McEvoy, A. (2005, September). *Teachers who bully students: Patterns and policy implications.* Paper presented at the Hamilton Fish Institute's Persistently Safe Schools Conference, Philadelphia. Retrieved from http://standupforstudents.com/blog/wp-content/uploads/2011/12/teachers_who_bully_students.239164537.pdf

McQuade, III, S. C., & Sampat, N. (2008). *Survey of internet and at-risk behaviors. Report of the Rochester Institute of Technology.* Rochester, NY: Rochester Institute of Technology. Retrieved from http://hdl.handle.net/1850/7652

Meyer-Adams, N., & Conner, B. T. (2008). School violence: Bullying behaviors and the psychosocial school environment in middle schools. *Children & Schools, 30*, 211–221.

Moe, J. L., Leggett, E. S., & Perera-Diltz, D. (2011). *School counseling for systemic change: Bullying and suicide prevention for LGBTQ youth.* Retrieved from http://counselingoutfitters.com/vistas/vistas11/Article_81.pdf

Nansel, T., Overpeck, M., Pilla, R. S., Ruan, W.J., Simmons-Morton, B., & Schmidt, P. (2001). Bullying behaviors among US youth. *Journal of American Medical Association, 285*, 2094–2100.

National Association of Pediatric Nurse Practitioners (NAPNAP). (2011). *Health risks and needs of gay, lesbian, bisexual, transgender, and questioning adolescents.* (National Association of Pediatric Nurse Practitioners' position statement.) Retrieved August 10, 2011 from http://www.napnap.org/PNPResources/Practice/PositionStatements.aspx

National Mental Health Association. (2002). What does gay mean? How to talk with kids about sexual orientation and prejudice. Retrieved from www.nmha.org/whatdoesgaymean

Neiman, S. (2011). *Crime, violence, discipline, and safety in U.S. public schools: Findings from the School Survey on Crime and Safety: 2009–10* (NCES 2011–320). U.S. Department of Education, National Center for Education Statistics. Washington, DC: U.S. Government Printing Office.

Nishina, A. (2004). A theoretical review of bullying: Can it be eliminated? In C. E. Sanders & G. D. Phye (Eds.), *Bullying: Implications for the classroom* (pp. 35–62). London: Elsevier Academic Press.

Nishioka, V., Coe, M., Burke, A., Hanita, M., & Sprague, J. (2011). *Student-reported overt and relational aggression and victimization in grades 3–8.* (Issues and Answers Report, REL 2011–No. 114). Washington DC: U.S. Department of Education, Institute of Education Sciences, National Center for Education Evaluation and Regional Assistance, Regional Educational Laboratory Northwest.

Northwest Regional Educational Laboratory (NWREL). (2001). *Schoolwide prevention of bullying.* Retrieved from http://www.nwrel.org/request/dec01/intro.html

NSPCC. (n.d.). *The NSPCC working definition of sexual bullying.* Retrieved on July 10, 2011, from http://www.nspcc.org.uk/Inform/resourcesforteachers/classroomresources/sexual_bullying_definition_wdf68769.pdf

O'Brennan, L. M., Bradshaw, C. P., & Sawyer, A. L. (2009). Examining developmental differences in the social-emotional problems among frequent bullies, victims, and bully/victims. *Psychology in the Schools, 46,* 100–115.

O'Connor, A. (2011, December 5). Sending of sexual images by minors isn't as prevalent as expected, study finds. *New York Times,* A15.

Ollove, M. (2010, April 28). Bullying and teen suicide: How do we adjust school climate? *The Christian Science Monitor.* Retrieved from http://www.csmonitor.com/USA/Society/2010/0428/Bullying-and-teen-suicide-How-do-we-adjust-school-climate

Olweus, D. (1993). *Bullying at school: What we know and what we can do.* New York: Blackwell.

Olweus, D. (2001). *Olweus' core program against bullying and antisocial behavior: A teacher handbook.* Bergen, Norway: Author.

Olweus, D., & Limber, S. P. (2010). Bullying in school: Evaluation and dissemination of the Olweus Bullying Prevention Program. *American Journal of Orthopsychiatry, 80,* 124–134.

Olweus, D., Limber, S. P., Flerx, V., Mullin, N., Riese, J., & Snyder, M. (2007). *Olweus Bullying prevention program: School-wide guide.* Center City, MN: Hazelden.

Olweus, D., Limber, S., & Mihalic, S. (1999). *Blueprints for violence prevention: Vol. 9. The bullying prevention program.* Boulder: Institute of Behavioral Science, University of Colorado.

Orpinas, P., & Horne, A. M. (2006). *Bullying prevention: Creating a positive school climate and developing social competence.* Washington, D.C.: American Psychological Association.

Parent Teacher Association of Connecticut, Inc. (2000). *Take action against bullying.* Retrieved on August 28, 2011, from http://www.mentalhealth.samhsa.gov/publications/allpubs/SVP-0056/

Parsons, L. (2005). *Bullied teacher: Bullied student—How to recognize the bullying culture in your school and what to do about it.* Markham, Canada: Pembroke Publishers Limited.

Patchin, J. W., & Hinduja, S. 2010. Cyberbullying and self-esteem. *Journal of School Health, 80,* 614–621.

Paul, A. M. (2011, June 20). Life after high school. *Time Magazine.* Retrieved on August 2, 2011, from http://www.time.com/time/magazine/article/0,9171,2076739,00.html

People for the American Way. (n.d.). *Big bullies: How the religious right is trying to make schools safe for bullies and dangerous for gay kids.* Retrieved on August 10, 2011, from http://www.pfaw.org/rww-in-focus/big-bullies-how-the-religious-right-trying-to-make-schools-safe-for-bullies-and-dangero

Pepler, D. (2001, May). Peer group dynamics and the culture of violence. In S. Hymel (Chair), *Culture of violence.* Symposium conducted at the annual meeting of the Royal Society of Canada (Academy II) and the Canadian Society for Studies in Education, Quebec City, Canada.

Peters, S. L. (2011, September 29). Dogs help schools lick bullies. *USA TODAY.* Retrieved from http://yourlife.usatoday.com/parenting-family/story/2011-09-28/Dogs-help-schools-lick-bullies/50592574/1

Petrosino, A., Guckenburg, S., DeVoe, J., & Hanson, T. (2010). *What characteristics of bullying, bullying victims, and schools are associated with increased reporting of bullying to school officials?* (Issues & Answers Report, REL 2010–No. 092). Washington, DC: U.S. Department of Education, Institute of Education Sciences.

The Pew Forum on Religion and Public Life. (2012). *U.S. Religious Landscape Survey.* Retrieved on January 10, 2012, from http://religions.pewforum.org/maps

Pew Research Center. (2010). *Generations 2010. Pew Internet & American Life Project* (a project of the Pew Research Center). Washington, DC: Author. Retrieved on December 5, 2011, from http://pewinternet.org/Reports/2010/Generations-2010.aspx

Porter, W., Plog, A., Jens, K., Garrity, C., Sager, N., & Jimerson, S. (2010). Bully-proofing your elementary school: Creating a caring community. In S. R. Jimerson, S. M. Swearer, & D. L. Espelage (Eds.), *Handbook of bullying in schools: An international perspective* (pp. 431–440). New York: Routledge.

Putnam, R. D., & Campbell, D. E. (2010). *American grace: How religion divides and unites us.* New York: Simon & Schuster.

Ragozzino, K., & O'Brien, M. U. (2009). *Social and emotional learning and bullying prevention.* Chicago: CASEL. Retrieved from http://casel.org/in-schools/bullying/

Rigby, K. (1995). What schools can do about bullying. *Professional Reading Guide for Educational Administrators, 17,* 1–5.

Rigby, K. (2002). *New perspectives on bullying.* London & Philadelphia: Jessica Kingsley Publishers.

Rivers, I., Chesney, T., & Coyne, I. (2011). Cyberbullying. In C. P. Monks & I. Coyne (Eds.), *Bullying in different contexts* (pp. 211–230). New York: Cambridge University Press.

Robers, S., Zhang, J., & Truman, J. (2010). *Indicators of school crime and safety: 2010* (NCES 2011-002/NCJ 230812). Washington, DC: National Center for Education Statistics, U.S. Department of Education, and Bureau of Justice Statistics, Office of Justice Programs, U.S. Department of Justice. Retrieved from http://nces.ed.gov/pubs2011/2011002.pdf

Rodgers, W. (2009, May 7). Religious bullying is a problem around the world. *The Christian Science Monitor*. Retrieved from www.csmonitor.com/layout/set/print/content/view/print/245997

Rodkin, P. C. (2011). Bullying and the power of peers. *Educational Leadership, 69*, 10–16.

Rodkin, P. C., & Hodges, E. V. E. (2003). Bullies and victims in the peer ecology: Four questions for psychologists and school professionals. *School Psychology Review, 32*, 384–400.

Roland, E. (2002). Bullying, depressive symptoms and suicidal thoughts. *Educational Research, 44*, 55–67.

Rosen, L. D., Cheever, N. A., & Carrier, L. M. (2008). The association of parenting style and child age with parental limit setting and adolescent MySpace behavior. *Journal of Applied Developmental Psychology, 29*, 459–471.

Rosenbluth, B. (2002). *Expect respect: A school-based program promoting safe and healthy relationships for youth*. Harrisburg, PA: National Resource Center on Domestic Violence.

Russell, S. T., & Joyner, K. (2002). Adolescent sexual orientation and suicide risk: Evidence from a national study. *American Journal of Public Health, 91*, 1276–1281.

Russell, S. T., Seif, H., & Truong, N. L. (2001). School outcomes of sexual minority youth in the United States: Evidence from a national study. *Journal of Adolescence, 24*, 111–127.

Sacks, J., & Salem, R. S. (2009). Victims without legal remedies: Why kids need schools to develop comprehensive anti-bullying policies. *Albany Law Review, 72*, 147–190.

Salin, D. (2003). Ways of explaining workplace bullying: A review of enabling, motivating and precipitating structures and processes in the work environment. *Human Relations, 56*, 1213–1232.

Salmivalli, C., Kärnä, A., & Poskiparta, E. (2010). From peer putdowns to peer support: A theoretical model and how it translated into a national anti-bullying program. In S. R. Jimerson, S. M. Swearer, & D. L. Espelage (Eds.), *Handbook of bullying in schools: An international perspective* (pp. 441–454). New York: Routledge.

Salmivalli, C., Lagerspetz, K., Bjorkqvist, K., Osterman, K., & Kaukiainen, A. (1996). Bullying as a group process: Participant roles and their relations to social status within the group. *Aggressive Behavior, 22*, 1–15.

Salmivalli, C., Voeten, M., & Poskiparta, E. (2011). Bystanders matter: Associations between reinforcing, defending, and the frequency of bullying behavior in classrooms. *Journal of Clinical Child & Adolescent Psychology, 40*, 668–676.

Sanders, C. J. (2010, October 2). Why anti-gay bullying is a theological issue: And the moral imperative of anti-bullying preaching, teaching, and activism. *Religion Dispatches*. Retrieved on July 11, 2011, from http://www.religiondispatches.org/archive/sexandgender/3479/why_anti-gay_bullying_is_a_theological_issue

Schrock, A., & Boyd, D. (2011). Problematic youth interaction online: Solicitation, harassment, and cyberbullying (pp. 368–396). In K. B. Wright & L. M. Webb (Eds.), *Computer-mediated communication in personal relationships*. New York: Peter Lang.

Schwartz, J. (2010, October 3). Bullying, suicide, punishment. *New York Times*, WK1.

Shah, N. (2011, November 2). Federal lawmakers weigh bullying-prevention proposals. *Education Week, 31*(10), pp. 14 & 17.

Shakeshift, C., Barber, E., Hergenrother, M., Johnson, Y. M., Mandel, L. S., & Sawyer, J. (1995). Peer harassment in schools. *Journal for a Just and Caring Education, 1*, 30–44.

Simonsen, B., Sugai, G., & Negron, M. (2008). Schoolwide positive behavior supports: Primary systems and practices. *TEACHING Exceptional Children, 40*, 32–40.

Slovak, K., & Singer, J. B. (2011). School social workers' perceptions of cyberbullying. *Children & Schools, 33*, 5–16.

Smith, P. K. (2011). Bullying in schools: Thirty years of research. In C. P. Monks & I. Coyne (Eds.), *Bullying in different contexts* (pp. 36–60). New York: Cambridge University Press.

Smith, P. K., Ananiadou, K., & Cowie, H. (2003). Interventions to reduce school bullying. *Canadian Journal of Psychiatry, 48*, 591–599.

Smith, P. K., & Shu, S. (2000). What good schools can do about bullying. Findings from a survey in English schools after a decade of research. *Childhood, 7*, 193–212.

Smokowski, P. R., & Kopasz, K. H. (2005). Bullying in school: An overview of types, effects, family characteristics, and intervention strategies. *Children and Schools, 27*, 101–109.

Sourander, A., Klomek, A. B., Ikonen, M., Lindroos, J., Luntamo, T., Koskelainen, M., et al. (2010). Psychosocial risk factors associated with cyberbullying among adolescents: A population-based study. *Archives of General Psychiatry, 67*, 720–728.

Sparks, S. D. (2011, November). Many teenagers can't distinguish harassment lines, research shows. *Education Week, 31*(11), pp. 1, 16–17.

Srabstein, J. C., & Leventhal, B. L. (2010). Prevention of bullying-related morbidity and mortality: A call for public health policies. *Bulletin of the World Health Organization, 88*, 403–403A.

Stein, N. D., & Mennemeier, K. A. (2011). *Addressing the gendered dimensions of harassment and bullying: What domestic and sexual violence advocates need to know.* Harrisburg, PA: The National Resource Center on Domestic Violence & The National Sexual Violence Resource Center. Retrieved on December 5, 2011, from http://www.vawnet.org

Stout, H. (2010, April 30). Antisocial networking? *The New York Times,* ST10.

Sullivan, E., & Keeney, E. (2008). *Teachers talk: School culture, safety, and human rights.* New York: National Economic and Social Rights Initiative (NESRI) and Teachers Unite.

Swearer, S. M., & Doll, B. (2001). Bullying in schools: An ecological framework. *Journal of Emotional Abuse, 2*, 7–24.

Swearer, S. M., & Espelage, D. L. (2011). Expanding the social-ecological framework of bullying among youth. In D. L. Espelage & S. M. Swearer (Eds.), *Bullying in North American schools* (2nd ed., pp. 3–10). New York: Routledge.

Swearer, S. M., Espelage, D. L., & Napolitano, S. A. (2009). *Bullying prevention and intervention: Realistic strategies for schools.* New York: Guilford.

Swearer, S., Espelage, D. L., Vaillancourt, T., & Hymel, S. (2010). What can be done about school bullying? Linking research to educational practice. *Educational Researcher, 39*, 38–47.

Swearer, S., Limber, S., & Alley, R. (2009). Developing and implementing an effective anti-bullying policy. In S. M. Swearer, D. L. Espelage, & S. A. Napolitano (Eds.),

Bullying prevention and intervention: Realistic strategies for schools (pp. 39–52). New York: The Guilford Press.

Sylvester, R. (2011). Teacher as bully: Knowingly or unintentionally harming students. *The Delta Kappa Gamma Bulletin, 77,* 42–45.

Szalacha, L. A. (2003). Safer sexual diversity climates: Lessons learned from an evaluation of Massachusetts safe schools program for gay and lesbian students. *American Journal of Education, 110,* 58–88.

Szalavitz, M. (2010, April 17). How not to raise a bully: The early roots of empathy. *Time Magazine.* Retrieved on May 2, 2011 from http://www.time.com/time/health/article/0,8599,1982190,00.html

Toomey, R. B., Ryan, C., Diaz, R. M., & Russell, S. T. (2011). High school gay–straight alliances (GSAs) and young adult well-being: An examination of GSA presence, participation, and perceived effectiveness. *Applied Developmental Science, 15,* 175–185.

Troop-Gordon, W., & Kopp, J. (2011). Teacher-child relationship quality and children's peer victimization and aggressive behavior in late childhood. *Social Development, 20,* 536–561.

Ttofi, M. M., & Farrington, D. P. (2009). What works in preventing bullying: Effective elements of anti-bullying programs. *Journal of Aggression, Conflict and Peace Research, 1,* 13–24.

Twemlow, S. W., & Fonagy, P. (2005). The prevalence of teachers who bully students in schools with differing levels of behavioral problems. *American Journal of Psychiatry, 162,* 2387–2389.

Twemlow, S. W., Fonagy, P., & Sacco, F. C. (2004). The role of the bystander in the social architecture of bullying and violence in schools and communities. *Annals of the New York Academy of Sciences, 1036,* 215–232.

Twemlow, S. W., Fonagy, P., Sacco, F., & Brethour, J. (2006). Teachers who bully students: A hidden trauma. *International Journal for Social Psychiatry, 52,* 187–198.

Twemlow, S. W., & Sacco, F. (2007). The prejudices of everyday life, with observations from field trials. In H. Parens, A. Mahfouz, S. W. Twemlow, & D. E. Scharff (Eds.), *The future of prejudice: Psychoanalysis and the prevention of prejudice* (pp. 237–254). Plymouth, UK: Rowman & Littlefield Publishers, Inc.

UCLA Center for Mental Health Services in Schools. (2011). *Addressing bullying: State guidance to districts and schools is both helpful and a missed opportunity.* Retrieved on November 3, 2011, from http://smhp.psych.ucla.edu/pdfdocs/bullying.pdf

Underwood, M. M., Rish-Scott, M., & Springer, J. (2011, September/October). Bullying and suicide risk: Building resilience. *Social Work Today, 11*(5), pp. 10–15.

Underwood, M. K., & Rosen, L. H. (2011). Gender & bullying. In D. L. Espelage & S. M. Swearer (Eds.), *Bullying in North American schools* (2nd ed., 13–22). New York: Routledge.

Underwood, M., Springer, J., & Scott, M. (2011). *Lifelines intervention.* Center City, MN: Hazelden Publishing.

Ungar, M. (2011). The social ecology of resilience: Addressing contextual and cultural ambiguity of a nascent construct. *American Journal of Orthopsychiatry, 81,* 1–17.

Unnever, J., & Cornell, D. (2004). Middle school victims of bullying: Who reports being bullied? *Aggressive Behavior, 30,* 373–388.

U.S. Department of Health and Human Services. (n.d.,a). *Best practices in bullying prevention and intervention. Stop bullying now resource kit.* Washington, DC: Author. Retrieved on June 10, 2011, from www.stopbullyingnow.hrsa.gov

U.S. Department of Health and Human Services. (n.d.,b). *Bullying among children and youth on perceptions and differences in sexual orientation. Stop bullying now resource kit.* Washington, DC: Author. Retrieved on June 12, 2011, from www.stopbullyingnow.hrsa.gov

U.S. Department of Health and Human Services. (n.d.,c). *Bullying among children and youth with disabilities and special needs. Stop bullying now resource kit.* Washington, DC: Author. Retrieved on June 12, 2011, from www.stopbullyingnow.hrsa.gov

U.S. Department of Health and Human Services. (n.d.,d). *Children who bully. Stop bullying now resource kit.* Washington, DC: Author. Retrieved on June 12, 2011, from www.stopbullyingnow.hrsa.gov

U.S. Department of Health and Human Services. (n.d.,e). *Myths about bullying. Stop bullying now resource kit.* Washington, DC: Author. Retrieved on June 12, 2011, from www.stopbullyingnow.hrsa.gov

Vaillancourt, T., Hymel, S., & McDougall, P., (2003). Bullying is power: Implications for school-based intervention strategies. *Journal of Applied School Psychology, 19,* 157–176.

Vaillancourt, T., Hymel, S., & McDougall, P. (2011). Why does being bullied hurt so much? Insights from neuroscience. In D. L. Espelage & S. M. Swearer (Eds.), *Bullying in North American schools* (2nd ed., pp. 23–33). New York: Routledge.

Vaillancourt, T., McDougall, P., Hymel, S., & Sunderani, S. (2010). Respect or fear? The relationship between power and bullying behavior. In S. R. Jimerson, S. M. Swearer, & D. L. Espelage (Eds.), *Handbook of bullying in schools: An international perspective* (pp. 211–222). New York: Routledge.

Vargas-Moll, I. (1991). A descriptive study of school induced stressors among Hispanic students. *Dissertation Abstracts International, 53*(01A), 0110. (UMI No. AAG9218121)

Vaughn, B. E., & Santos, A. J. (2007). An evolutionary/ecological account of aggressive behavior and trait aggression in human children and adolescents. In P. H. Hawley, T. D. Little, & P. C. Rodkin (Eds.), *Aggression and adaptation: The bright side to bad behavior* (pp. 31–64). Mahwah, NJ: Lawrence Erlbaum Associates, Publishers.

Viadero, D. (2010, May 19). Studies probe "ecology" of bullying. *Education Week, 29*(32), pp. 1, 18–19.

Vreeman, R. C., & Carroll, A. E. (2007). A systematic review of school-based interventions to prevent bullying. *Archives of Pediatric Adolescent Medicine, 161,* 78–88.

Wang, M. C., Haertel, G. D., & Walberg, H. J. (1997). Learning influences. In H. J. Walberg & G. D. Haertel (Eds.), *Psychology and educational practice* (pp. 199–211). Berkeley, CA: McCuthan.

Walton, G. (2004). Bullying and homophobia in Canadian schools. *Journal of Gay & Lesbian Issues in Education, 1,* 23–36.

Wang, J., Iannotti, R. J., & Nansel, T. R. (2009). School bullying among adolescents in the United States: Physical, verbal, relational, and cyber. *Journal of Adolescent Health, 45,* 368–375.

Whitted, K. S., & Dupper, D. R. (2008). Do teachers bully students? Findings from a survey of students in an alternative school setting. *Education and Urban Society, 40,* 329–341.

Wisconsin Clearinghouse for Prevention Resources. (n.d.). *Bullying: What we know.* Retrieved on June 2, 2011, from http://wch.uhs.wisc.edu

Wiser, M. (2011, August 21). Iowa schools will pilot new bullying policy. *Sioux City Journal.* Retrieved on September 8, 2011, from http://siouxcityjournal.com/news/state-and-regional/iowa/iowa-schools-will-pilot-new-bullying-policy/article_7cc5a717-e1da-560e-bfa9-d5f7ab63f6a9.html

Wolak, J., Finkelhor, D., Mitchell, K., & Ybarra, M. (2008). Online "predators" and their victims: Myths, realities, and implications for prevention and treatment. *American Psychologist, 63,* 111–128.

Woolfolk Hoy, A., & Weinstein, C. S. (2006). Student and teacher perspectives on classroom management. In C. M. Evertson & C. S. Weinstein (Eds.), *Handbook of classroom management: Research, practice, and contemporary issues* (pp. 181–219). Mahwah, NJ: Erlbaum.

Ybarra, M. L., Diener-West, M., & Leaf, P. J. (2007). Examining the overlap in Internet harassment and school bullying: Implications for school intervention. *Journal of Adolescent Health, 41,* S42–S50.

Ybarra, M., Espelage, D. L., & Martin, S. (2011). Unwanted sexual & harassing experiences: From school to text messaging. In D. L. Espelage & S. M. Swearer, *Bullying in North American schools* (2nd ed., pp. 62–72). New York: Routledge.

You, S., Furlong, M. J., Felix, E., Sharkey, J. D., Tanigawa, D., & Green, J. G. (2008). Relations among school connectedness, hope, life satisfaction, and bullying victimization. *Psychology in the Schools, 45,* 446–460.

Zelikoff, W. (1990). A retrospective study of school related stressors of educators. *Dissertation Abstracts International, 51*(08A), 2690. (UMI No. AAG9100360)

Zubrzycki, J. (2011, October 19). Lawmakers take aim at bullying: New measures adopted in nearly half the states. *Education Week, 31*(8), pp. 1 & 16.

Index